The Homeschool Highway:


How To Navigate Your Way

Without Getting Carsick


By Amy Dingmann

# Table of Contents

# Introduction:

## Buckle Up, Baby

Ah, the road of homeschooling. It's a lovely ride filled with togetherness, freedom, and the knowledge that you journey down the road in whatever style you feel is right.

But consider yourself forewarned. As lovely as the drive is, you'll probably get carsick along the way.

Years ago, when I started my research of homeschooling, I was convinced it would be The Choice for our family. I presented to my husband a safe, happy, peaceful, fail proof vision of what homeschooling would be (cue choir of angels), and he agreed we should give it a try.

Now to my knowledge I wasn't lying. Because safe, happy, peaceful and fail proof (and again, the choir of angels) was what my many hours of research had turned up. But the farther we got down the road of homeschooling, the harder things became. We tripped upon many issues packaged up inside the homeschooling territory that I'd seen *nowhere* on the map I'd bought for the trip.  I found myself irritated far more than occasionally, and it was completely unrelated to how to get the kids interested in Ancient Egypt. What was more disturbing, however, was when I turned to other homeschoolers for help, I was made to feel like I must be doing something wrong if I was frustrated.

It just *had* to be me, right? My research online, in homeschool groups, and in books had told me homeschooling was the absolute perfect educational choice! It is academically superior! It strengthens your family and brings people together! And if you're not feelin' it, you are homeschooling incorrectly. Right?

I say *wrong*.

I want you to do something.

Right now.

I want you to take a minute to think about all the things you struggle with about homeschooling. The things that are hard. The things you've been biting off your tongue not to say.

I want you to tell them, right now, to me.

That's right. Let it fly. No one will even care you're yelling at your book or e-reader. Don't worry about those people. Just go ahead and tell me about all those rough spots. All those potholes along the road of homeschooling that you've found yourself jarred by. Get it off your chest.

There.

Feel better?

Homeschooling is hard. Really hard. The problem is no one talks about the hard parts. We talk about the freedom and peace and how we all love each other and our kids scored a thousand times higher on those tests than the public school kids.

We talk about the perfection of homeschooling. We skip over the hard parts. Or we talk about them very little, barely scratching the surface of the things that keep us up at night, wondering if we've made the wrong choice for our family. We make jokes about how frustrated we are. We're always just kidding.

We talk about the idealized homeschool when we need to be comfortable enough to talk about the real homeschool.

I'm a bit of a rebel, I guess. I'm going to admit right now there are days, weeks...dare I say months...when homeschooling is infinitely less than enjoyable. I'm also a rebel because I think it's important you know that some days are just like that.

That's just how it goes.

And it's ok.

Every decision has some pros and some cons. Every thing you encounter, no matter how fabulous, can bring struggles or rough patches. Police officers who like the excitement of car chases also have to deal with a lot of time spent in a car, bored out of their mind, waiting for something to happen. A writer might have an occasional lazy day spent with her muse in a coffee shop, but also deals with deadlines, unreliable interviewees, broken contracts, and lots of rejection. Lottery winners get a whole blob of money, but also have to change their phone number because friends come out of the woodwork and charities won't leave them alone. That's called Real Life...and homeschooling is no different.

Don't get me wrong. It's *great* to be a homeschooler! I love those days when I'm kneading bread dough and my son is reading me chapters of some novel at the table. I like it when we're doing music class (a jam session of various instruments around the campfire) or wildlife biology (watching the deer, fox, and coyote run down the gravel road in front of our house). There are lots of days I love.

But homeschoolers have days that aren't quite loveable. Homeschoolers have Stuff they've got to deal with. Extended family and friends who don't agree with their decision. Personality Clashes between people in their own household. Mom's complete loss of self because she's always surrounded by children. That tired socialization question that everyone seems to ask but no one really understands.

And that's just for starters.

We have a lot to deal with. Our plates are full. And it's sometimes hard to eat and drive at the same time.

## Disclaimer from the Author

I'd really like to write the One Great Book About Homeschooling.

But I can't. And here's why: Homeschoolers are all different.

Not everything in this book will apply to you. There are many different types of homeschoolers, and it would be impossible to write a book only containing issues that apply to every family who chooses to home educate. The beauty of choosing home education is that things can be (and are!) different from one household to the next. My goal here is simply to shed light on some of the issues people don't always talk about (but still struggle with) and suggest ways to deal with them. I am not a guru. I don't have all the answers. Take from this book what works for you, and feel free to leave what doesn't for someone else.

## Another Disclaimer from the Author

I live on a multi-generational farm. My kids have farm animals and chores.

My husband, financial supporter of the Clucky Dickens Farm Homeschool, works nights in law enforcement.

Our original reasons for homeschooling were academics, hyperactivity, and my husband's work schedule.

I live in a state that requires annual testing.

I'm telling you these random bits of information because each nugget is another clue about why we've chosen to homeschool the way we have. It means that my kids have a certain time they need to wake up by (goats get really loud if they are hungry). It means that my kids need to take their noisy science experiments out of the house if Dad happens to be sleeping.

Does it mean if you are different that your way is wrong? Not at all. If your way works for you, it's perfect. It is important when discussing a lifestyle so deeply based in personal choice and opinion, that we have some idea *where* that person's choices and opinions came from. I've known people who chose to homeschool strictly because of food allergies, and had other homeschoolers look down their nose at them for using online public school curriculum...as if they are ignoring some secret creed!

We need to remember that the *way* we homeschool has to do with *why* we homeschool. Our learning environments are going to look different. Our schedules are going to look different. Our days are going to look different. And it's ok, because *different* is kind of the point of choosing to homeschool.

### One more disclaimer

My family does not operate under a homeschooling label or category. This book is not to bash or celebrate one label or the other. I don't consider myself an unschooler or a classical educator, although through my blog and speaking I've had a lot of *other people* label what we do. That has never been self-imposed. In the beginning of our homeschooling journey, we'd try to paste one of the labels above our homeschool, but we had a *more awesome* and *ultimately cooler* homeschooler inform us that no, in fact, we weren't a (fill in the blank) because we didn't (fill in the blank).

I don't have enough time to argue about what word I should call myself. I'm too busy living this life with my kids. (Frankly, people who **do** have the time to argue about labels worry me a bit.) We've been homeschooling long enough that the lines have blurred between the categories and labels anyway. Ultimately (and most importantly) my kids don't care what we call ourselves, so neither do I.

If you love this book, great! Tell everyone you know, including their brothers and sisters. Blog about it. Tweet about it. Update your facebook status, and press like. Consider leaving a review on Amazon.

My goal with this book is to make you deeply contemplate your homeschooling journey – whether you are five years into it, almost done, or just considering it. Even if this book does nothing more than help your family decide that homeschooling isn't Your Choice, that's ok. Homeschooling is all about choice, so your choice is perfect. My purpose here is to clarify home education and show the ways it can play itself out – the good, the bad, *and* the ugly.

And so, we're off! We head out to explore the road of homeschooling – everything from scenic wayside rests to tire popping potholes along the way.

Buckle up, baby. You're in for a ride.

# Chapter 1

## Flexibility: Blessing...or Curse?

So here you are on the road of homeschooling, ready to go. Your Minivan of Awesome is pointed toward the goal. You've got your map. You've got your cooler of food. You've got all the educational DVDs and CDs you can handle. You're ready to rock.

The first thing you've got to figure out is *how* you want to get to where you're going.

*What?* You ask. *But we're on the Homeschooling Highway! Isn't that how I'm getting there?*

Well, yes. But the Homeschooling Highway is actually made up of millions of different types of roads. They all lead to the same place but are very *very* different in how you travel. You just need to decide which is best for your carload of kids.

There's the dirt road where you're bound to get dusty, but there are many treasures to be found.

There are side streets that go through lovely neighborhoods.

There are teeny minimum maintenance roads which sometimes dead end.

There are roads that are known for their scenic views, but they make for a longer trip.

There are roads that are straight, narrow, and fast...but there's not much to look at.

There are all sorts of roads that are part of the Homeschooling Highway.

And choosing your road is just one of many choices you get to make.

You don't have to talk to a homeschooling parent very long before you'll hear them gush about the fabulous flexibility of homeschooling. It's a lifestyle where school can fit into life, instead of life fitting into school. And when you stop to think about that, it's an amazing concept. Somewhat foreign to most of us, but so very appealing!

Homeschooling, by its very nature, is the epitome of flexibility. It draws to it those people who want choices and options. It can be intoxicating, especially to new homeschoolers, to think they can set up their day however they want, using whatever curriculum they want, following whatever path of learning works best for their family.

Flexibility, and the choices within homeschooling that make it what it is, can truly give your family a rich and varied experience down the road you travel. If you're willing to be flexible with curriculum, learning methods, activities, groups and other things you bring into your day, you're really going blow the roof off of your children's educational experience.

In homeschooling, you can keep things new and fresh. No one wants to eat the same thing for lunch everyday. And no one wants to learn history or art or writing in the same way everyday, either. In homeschooling, you have the option to toss things up like a lovely educational salad, and serve it up differently. Everyday.

There are always options. I have one child who loved learning his multiplication tables through an online math game. My other child just wanted to learn math from a book. One child thinks reading about history aloud is the most exciting way to learn, while my other child just wants to watch well done history documentaries. I have one child who wants to touch everything he learns and I have another child who just wants to hear it.

It's great to have options. It's great to be flexible!

There are options in homeschooling that just aren't available with other educational choices. You even have options for how to deal with the weather!

We live in Minnesota, and winter has a way of hanging on for almost forever. One particularly rough year, we waited for what seemed like an eternity for winter to give up and die. That season that had been one of the coldest and snowiest in recent memory, and we had cabin fever something fierce. My homeschooling men were itching to be outside, but at 35 degrees below zero, there wasn't much to do but time how long it took your teeth to start chattering (and we'd already documented that.) So we stayed locked up inside, ever hopeful for a change.

And then one March day, it happened. The sun came out. The temperature shot up to a whopping 20 degrees, and the boys were itching to try out their homemade snowboards.

We had a pile of math and spelling to work on. The boys were supposed to be finishing up their classic novels they'd chosen to read. But seriously? This weather called for a celebration. We tossed the books aside, announced no school, and spent the majority of the day messing up the blinding white blanket of snow in our backyard.

Thank goodness we've got the option for flexibility.

Yes, flexibility is wonderful and incredible and completely amazing.

However...

...and you're probably not going to believe this, but...

...there comes a time when the freedom and flexibility of homeschooling can be...well, completely overwhelming. Way too much. Completely out of control.

Yeah. I know. Impossible, right?

But hear me out.

There are four ways I've seen homeschooling flexibility turn into a tangled up mess.

**One: I'm a crow, and I get distracted by shiny things.**

With homeschooling, you get flexibility in not only what, but how your kids learn. You're able to go beyond the four walls of a classroom, blast through the ceiling and explore the whole wide world.

Sounds fabulous, right?

Not if you're a crow.

See, the great thing about homeschooling now (as opposed to even 10 years ago) are the many options for the "what and how and when" of gettin' it done.

But.

The really *hard* thing about homeschooling now is...you guessed it: the many options for the "what and how and when" of gettin' it done. In homeschooling, every choice has the potential to be shiny and distracting. Everything, especially when you have *young* kids, looks fun. Or amazing. Or perfect. There isn't enough time in the day to do everything you could. But that doesn't stop a few crazy souls from trying.

A parent (maybe me, but I'm not pointing any fingers...) decides upon the perfect homeschooling road to travel upon. And then she (again, maybe me, but we don't need to be specific...) might talk to another homeschooling parent and figure out a different road. And then that same mom (ok, it's totally me) might read a book...or see someone's product...or look at someone's blog...and figure out another path. And then she talks to someone else and sees a neat project. A really cool thing. An awesome place to visit. And now we're on a completely different path, doing a completely different thing, and...

Oh, gosh. Someone stop me!

Depending on how your family deals with an insane amount of mind-changing will determine how well this works out for you. It didn't work for us. I remember my oldest watching me whiz through a glob of activities that were all really great, but totally disjointed. He looked right at me and said, "Mom, I don't get how this fits with what you were just talking about five minutes ago."

Whoa. Might be time to back off a bit.

One of the struggles of flexibility is determining for your family where flexibility ends and chaos begins. It's different for every carload of homeschoolers, and it doesn't matter what works for the minivan that is making faces at you in the left lane. What matters is what makes *your* car go.

It's great to have choices. It's great to have options. They give you different approaches to get things done. But if you have too many choices or options, sometimes you just become the babbling idiot in the front of the car, not knowing where to drive or where you were supposed to be going anyway.

## Two: Not every kid thrives on freedom.

Our family merged onto the Homeschool Highway back in 2007. I believed if I just opened the door and let my kids run free (dodging traffic, of course), they'd burrow themselves into their interests and all would be well with the world. I really wanted to subscribe to a (much) less structured way of schooling. At the time, we lived on a fabulous 13 acres of woods, swamp, and yard. We had chickens. We had gardens. Think of all we could learn in our lovely days of hanging out! I laid out books on various subjects, had beautiful projects available, and I opened the door to learning *wide*. Nothing was off limits.

Unfortunately, a certain child didn't like that idea. At all.

Anyone who has more than one child in the minivan knows that conflicting personalities abound in the vehicle. In our car, we've got two boys who sit on opposite ends of the spectrum, regardless of what topic you're discussing.

One of my sons thought freedom was great. Flexibility was awesome. What were we talking about again? Peanut butter sandwiches? Oh yeah. And bring me another DS game. Can I get a dog? Can I stay up late? Why can't you see the stars in the daytime again? I really like Legos.

He's flexible.

My other son was different. Although he liked being able to choose topics he was interested in, he couldn't get over the not knowing of what we were doing, how long it would last, and what we were doing next. He wanted continuity. His analytical mind had a need-to-know. Concrete details and schedules were his thing, and he didn't like not being told.

Flexible, he is not.

So you can see how our original traffic dodging plan wasn't going to quite work out. If I couldn't give a certain child the exact hour/minute/second we'd be journeying to the next destination on the map, we were in for a child sized freak-out on the side of the road.

But wait! I had this all planned out to not have a plan! And now you want me to be flexible about...flexibility?

**Three: When things get hard, pull the card.**

"Mom?" my son said. "I'm not finding much interest in math anymore."

He twirled around in the office chair, staring at the ceiling.

I'm not sure what he wanted me to say. I'm guessing it was along the lines of *ok, then don't do math.* But math is the subject I'm a stickler about, so instead, I answered *bummer*.

A couple days later, while he was doing *anything but* the math in front of him, he said, "You know...I really just don't like math anymore."

I told him that could be a real problem, since he had about eight more years of math to learn.

The next day he tried a new one: "Mom, I suck at math."

"You do not *suck* at math," I reassured him. "You hardly ever get any of your math problems wrong."

"Yeah, but it takes me f-o-r-e-v-e-r to get done."

I knew what was happening. He wanted me to pull the flexibility card.

*Definition: Flexibility Card – 1) Changing what you're doing because it's no longer fun/interesting/pertinent/working for someone in the family. Ex. Amy pulled the flexibility card because the grammar program was lame.*

My oldest son doesn't care for math. Never has, and probably never will. I have two ways I can deal with this:

A) I can change math curriculums. Again. Maybe the five we've already tried aren't the ticket. The next one could be. I should be flexible enough to figure out what curriculum is going to make it click for him.

B) I could accept that math isn't entirely fun. And short of shoving a Butterfinger or Snickers in my son's mouth every time he successfully solves a math equation, I'm not sure it's going to get any more exciting.

The real issue is my oldest is a bit of an overachiever. He slants (heavily) towards the perfectionist side. At the beginning of our current curriculum, he could complete the entire lesson in five minutes. Now it takes him twenty. The math is getting harder (as it should) and he has to stop. and. think. of. how. to. do. it.

And he doesn't like that.

*Not at all.*

So how does a flexible homeschooler deal with that, and the many situations like it that come up?

Dear fellow drivers of Minivans of Awesome, sometimes you'll find yourself in a situation that has nothing to do with methodology, curriculum choice, or how creative we can be. In the above math scenario, the issue at hand doesn't even have anything to do with math. It *does*, however, have a lot to do with getting older and the simple act of progressing academically. Mostly, it's about accepting a challenge and sticking with something that's difficult. And no matter how you slice it, you can't always solve that one with the flexibility card. Sometimes you just have to do it. In fact, if you pull the flexibility card too much, you have the potential to make this problem worse.

Um...yay flexibility?

## Four: The dark side of flexibility

It was the perfect idea. We would reserve the gym at the local community center and hold an open hour for all the homeschoolers in the area. But when the call was placed to reserve the time slot, the answer from administration was no.

"No? Should we pick a different time?"

"No," was the solid response. "We do not reserve time slots to homeschoolers unless we have a certain amount of attendees paid up front."

"Why not?"

"Because, in our experience, homeschoolers are known for not showing up."

The longer I am involved in the homeschooling community, the more I see this happening. It's *modus operandi* for some homeschooling families to not show up to something because a better offer came along. This often comes in the form of:

*Gee. I know we said we'd be at that art class, but it was such a nice day, we decided we'd have a picnic in the backyard instead.*

*Sorry, I know I said we'd show up for the 11:00 tour, but it was so cold and the kids didn't want to go outside.*

*Oh, was today the science fair? I totally forgot because (giggle) we were walking down by the river...have you been down there lately?*

*I know we didn't make it to the museum again, but you know, we've got to be flexible.*

Apparently there's mass confusion within a sector of the homeschooling population regarding the definition of flexible.

Flexible means adaptable. Adjustable. Changeable. Modifiable.

Flexible does not mean don't follow through.

Flexible does not mean chaos.

Flexible does not mean failure to commit.

Ah, commitment! Class, let's review:

*Definition: Commit – 1) to pledge or engage oneself. To stay the course. 2) to bind or obligate, as by pledge or assurance; a promise. Ex. Amy will commit to having her children at the art class on Friday.*

Now I'm not talking about when your child pukes in the car and you have to pull over. And I'm not talking about when you can't navigate the roads because they're covered in ice. There is a difference between not showing up because your car wouldn't start, and never showing up because you always change your plans at the last minute. At some point, a failure to show up is just *not following through* on what you said you would do.

Now, don't get me wrong. It is your right as a homeschooling parent to not show up. You're a rebel, and no one is going to tell you what to do. But I do want to ask anyone who has taken flexibility to a chaotic level: what is the benefit, and what is it teaching your kids?

I have to ask because, well…we're homeschoolers. And what it's *teaching the kids* is kinda the whole point.

We have to be careful to not go overboard and abuse our flexibility. It's giving people the impression we're all scatterbrained freak parents with an inability to commit. It reflects poorly on our Minivan of Awesome.

I remember being at a homeschool gathering and running into a lovely homeschooling mom I hadn't seen in about a year. We got to talking and I admitted that I felt confused about what our path as homeschoolers was.

"I feel like I never know where we're headed. Just about the time I think I get things figured out with the kids, they go and do something completely different and I have to change everything."

Her Minivan of Awesome had been on the road of homeschooling much longer than mine. She just looked at me with an understanding smile and said, "Yep. As soon as you think you've found center....center moves."

Exactly.

The road of homeschooling when you have a five year old is completely different than when you have a 14 year old. The road of homeschooling when you're the parent of one child is totally changed when you become the parent of four. Or ten.

It seems as though these points would be obvious, but when we're in the middle of it, wondering why things have suddenly changed or gotten harder, we sometimes don't see what's right in front of our face.

Homeschooling morphs and changes as your family morphs and changes, and it should. That's what makes homeschooling so great. It can snuggle up to the new shape or direction your family is taking. It's not rigid. It works with what you do.

But you have to *let it* work.

I've been homeschooling long enough now to know there are times of the year when we (for reasons specific to our family) need to be really rigid and structured in what we're doing. And there are other times of the year when we just can't and don't. I've been on the road long enough to know that sometimes we are really hands-on and sometimes we aren't. Sometimes we're all about field trips. Sometimes we're all about building things. Sometimes we bust out worksheets. It depends on what is working at the moment and what the kids are needing and asking for.

But, oh gosh...I remember when we first merged onto the Homeschooling Highway. Every time we'd hit one of these places where we needed to shift or morph, I was pretty sure the world was ending, there was something wrong with our family, and our Minivan of Awesome was uncontrollably skidding towards the nearest cliff.

Homeschooling works because it's moldable to the cracks and crevices that Life has. And a concept I've had to add to my entire understanding of flexibility is the "life changes" that homeschooling can support aren't always the positive ones.

Life is always changing, and we like to embrace that as homeschoolers when it means we can claim flexibility in a good and exciting way, like suddenly taking two weeks off for a trip around the state. You know, the part of flexibility that makes people jealous.

But life changing doesn't always refer to the great things, it also refers to the things that are hard. The things you didn't want to change. Sometimes flexible simply means we have options. However, we might not necessarily like all the options we have.

If we've chosen a certain lane of the Homeschooling Highway, and it doesn't end up working for our family, we get to be flexible and change it. Does that mean that you, as the homeschooling parent are necessarily going to be thrilled about that change? Nope.

But hey. You're being *flexible*.

Sometimes flexibility means having the ability to change something you were so sure was going to work but it completely blew up in your face and messed up all your plans. We tend to focus on the fact that the plan blew up, not the fact that we had many options for how to deal with its aftermath.

But hey. We're *flexible*.

When we started homeschooling, my husband spent his work week living an hour away, and would come home on his long stretches of days off. We thought the perfect way to set up our homeschool life was to do the less exciting/more work things when Dad had to be gone, and save the fun things for when he could be home with us.

And we seriously didn't see how that could fail.

At first it was great, and we did some amazingly special things while Dad was able to be with us. But it didn't take long for the kids to put two and two together: when Dad was home, it meant fun. When he wasn't, it meant work.

It also didn't take long before that division of fun/work became an issue between mom and dad.

The kids saw me as the workhorse (driving them along to do math and spelling) while Dad got to be there for every field trip, every awesome science experiment, and every hands-on building project we could muster. When I wanted to do something that fell under the "fun category", they thought we had to *wait for Dad*. When it was time for us to work, I got groans and eye rolls and *when is Dad coming home.*

Aww. I love you, too.

This set up did *not* work. And no one was happy about the fact it didn't work, because it was supposed to be the perfect set up for our family.

So we had to be flexible. We morphed things. Sometimes field trips happened when Dad couldn't be there. Sometimes Dad helped out with the math lesson. It wasn't what we'd planned as our set up, but it ended up being our set up.

Thank goodness for flexibility, right?

At this point, our family has been homeschooling long enough we don't get too cozy with center. Or we might get cozy, but we don't hold on to it so tightly that when center moves (because it always does), we're left standing on the shoulder of Homeschooling Highway, completely stuck in the mud. Flexibility is the piece of good fortune which, when used in the best way for your family, can knock the socks off your educational experience. Make peace with what flexibility is, where your line between it and chaos lies, and let that Minivan of Awesome move forward!

## Chapter 2

## Sometimes I Don't Want To Be With My Kids

I adore my children and I've built a significant amount of my life around them. But I'm going to let you in on a little secret.

Sometimes I don't want to be with my kids.

Know what's even crazier?

Sometimes my kids don't want to be with me.

Shocking, isn't it?

When we all hopped in the car on this homeschooling gig, I really thought we'd be happy to sit together, boppin' along to a radio station we all agreed on while we played some silly game about license plates.

I can count on one hand the days that fantasy has been fulfilled.

Being the mom and the teacher is great, and I'm quite thankful that I can say I do both. (Especially since there was a time when I was pretty sure this homeschooling gig wasn't going to fly with the financial supporter of Clucky Dickens Homeschool.) But homeschooling is stressful. My children will try things and test me in ways they would never dream of doing with other people. I know it has been said that children will test the people they love and feel the most comfortable with. I don't know if that is supposed to give me some sort of warm fuzzy feeling or what, but somedays…I'm just not feelin' it.

In fact, I would go so far as to say that since we made the decision to homeschool, my children have actually located Mom buttons to push that I did not have before. Buttons that grew when we became homeschoolers, labeled *New And Special Ways To Annoy Mom*.

See what I mean about that warm fuzzy feeling?

I think our problem is that we get into this homeschooling thing and forget there are two different kinds of homeschooling. There is the idea of homeschooling, and then there is actual homeschooling. The idea of homeschooling is fuzzy and warm and ideal. Actual homeschooling is completely different and we often forget what the dailyness of being both mom and teacher (actual homeschooling) really requires.

Wait. I know what you are thinking. You're saying "But being mom and being teacher and the same exact thing."

I know what you're getting at. I really do. I taught my kids to walk and talk and eat their cereal without mashing it all over their face and I did that all as a mom. So it's all the same thing, right?

No. I don't think so. Because there are days when I have threatened to lock myself in the bathroom and scream into the mirror "Today I just want to be mom!"

There *is* a difference between mom and teacher when it comes to homeschooling. As mom, I get to tell my son he needs braces and can't eat popcorn until next Halloween. I get to ask my youngest to clean up his not-so-secret toothpaste artwork on the bathroom mirror. I get to ask how long the boys think they can forget to feed the dog before he dies. I get to wonder if they're ever going to clean out their horse's stall without me reminding them. As mom AND teacher, I get to do all those things, and then slap a smile on my face and say "Hey, let's all hold hands and learn about the power of long division!"

If my children were in public school, we'd have those completely normal mom/child disagreements...and then they'd leave on the big yellow bus for 9 hours. We'd all have time to process what had happened. We'd have time to cool off.

In homeschooling, we don't necessarily have that separation. You don't have that cool down time. You *or* the kids. Issues happen on top of issues...on top of issues...and then there is math....and everything builds on top of what just happened ten minutes ago. You can't get away from it.

And that can be tough.

Yes, the togetherness teaches us all that we have to be way bigger people than we probably are, and we learn really good conflict resolution skills. But while you're in the middle of that togetherness, it can be really frustrating.

Sometimes overwhelming.

I remember a particularly tough week for the boys and me. We really needed to not be in the car together any longer. I moped around and struggled with what this meant. We were supposed to be growing closer as a family, not be at each other's throats. I was obviously a homeschooling failure.

My mother enlightened me, however, by asking that I consider what life would have been like if I had been homeschooled.

"Oh, it would have been great", I fantasized, pointing out the billions of things I could have done academically; the crazy things I would have had time to experience.

But that wasn't what she'd meant.

"Would you have wanted to be with your sister all day?" she asked.

My sister?

All day?

I love my sister as all sisters love their sisters. But be with her *all day*? Everyday? For everything?

Let me spork my eyeballs out.

And suddenly, with that realization, I figured out why my kids and I were climbing the sides of the car with frustration.

We weren't failures. We just needed a decent amount of time apart.

It turns out this is a problem in a lot of homeschools. It's another example of how the same thing that makes homeschooling so great - togetherness - can also be one of its downfalls.

I had the opportunity to teach an upper grades poetry class at a co-op we were involved in. One of the pieces we worked on was about our honest feelings of being homeschooled. At the time, I had very young homeschooled kids and was still thinking Homeschool Utopia was possible.

*I love being homeschooled,* one girl in the class said, *but I wish my parents knew I needed time away from them and my siblings.*

*I love my family,* said another, *but I just need time to breathe without them around.*

Do you see a pattern here?

Our real issue is that we hop on the Homeschooling Highway with the goal in mind and forget about the daily ins and outs of how to get there. We think about the Awesome, but we forget about all the driving that it takes to be in the Minivan.

We also forget about the simple fact that as we're all rolling down the road in that Minivan of Awesome, there might be plenty of room for the physical bodies...but not the personalities.

As kids get older, they are figuring out who they are and their personalities are becoming more defined. That's really awesome to watch...and sometimes really hard to watch. Sometimes the personalities fit together nicely, other times not so much. Our joy as homeschooling parents is to see if we can make that all work out.

Sometimes we clash with other members in the minivan because we're so different. I have one darling rider who would like nothing more than to have me pull over so he can moonwalk down the shoulder of the highway and have people wave at him.

He and I are different creatures, entirely. He's spur of the moment. He's indecisive. He's literally goes until he crashes...and even then you can't slow him down or shut him up.

Our brains work completely differently. One day, while trying on shoes, I asked him if the one he had on fit well. He screwed up his face and yelled, "No! There's a drop off at the end of this one!" I asked him to explain what he meant. He asked me why I didn't get what he was talking about. I asked him why he was talking about water (drop offs) while we were trying on shoes. He asked me why I didn't understand that drop off meant that when he picked his foot up, the back of the shoe *dropped off.* I asked him why he couldn't just say the shoe was too big. I was still crabby and frustrated when he bopped away to run through the yard, barefoot. He had completely forgotten the entire thing before it was even over.

Yes, our brains work differently.

Can you see why time in the Minivan of Awesomeness might get a little...strained sometimes?

We do not, however, only clash with people because they are different from ourselves. Sometimes we butt heads because we're too much alike. Children have an amazing way of mirroring the qualities of yourself that you've squashed down or thought you made peace with, but totally didn't.

One of the discussions I often have with my oldest is how, even though he'd much rather sit in the corner and read, he can't spend 365 days a year doing that. He'd like to be a hermit in the Northwoods of Minnesota, but as a nine year old boy, I'd like to give him occasional tastes of different things, people, and experiences.

Getting him to agree to things that involve other carloads of people is literally like pulling teeth. He doesn't see the point of large gatherings of people and gets completely freaked out when he's in them.

We verbally scrap about this, me mostly fearing that he'll be the poster child for *Children Who are Homeschooled Don't Associate With Other People*. As a mom, I want him to play nice with others. As a mom, I want him to be social. As a mom, I want him to be out there.

But oh my goodness, that kid is me.

If I'm honest with myself (and you) I would have to admit the entire reason we moved out to the middle of nowhere is because...well, it's the middle of nowhere. I love that we see three cars a day. I love that if people don't call for directions, they will never figure out how to get to our home. I love the time I get to sit and write...or read...and I could easily spend all day inside my head without thinking to come out for anything. I love that we homeschool, and just maybe it had a little to do with the fact that we could do our own thing and not be bothered by anyone else.

Gosh. I sound like my kid.

And he sounds like me.

Not long ago my husband came home with tickets he'd received to an event. A friend couldn't go and passed the VIP tickets along to him. He started telling me about it, asking if I wanted to go...and I was fine...until he mentioned something about the event drawing a crowd of a thousand people...

"Nope," I said. "I don't want to go. Too many people."

My oldest was standing right next to me.

And he smirked.

Yep. Like mother, like son.

All of this clashing of personalities and togetherness and daily in and out can make the ride in the minivan tense at times. We're climbing the sides of the van, clawing at the seats for a little time apart. And sometimes feeling badly for wanting to get away makes the feeling worse. But snagging those moments apart is perfectly ok. It's healthy for you and your family to have alone time.

My husband is great at knowing when I need a break from the kids and when they need a break from me. Occasionally my husband will grab my car keys, steer me towards the door with orders he doesn't want to see me until after the kids are in bed.

Yep, he totally kicks me out of the house. And off the property.

At first I used to be offended by this. I used to stress out thinking it was him saying *You need to go because you obviously can't handle these kids and you're a failure as a homeschooling mom.* But that's not what it was at all. My husband is a smartie and knows that if mom gets time from the kids and the kids get time from mom, the Minivan of Awesome will be happy again when everyone finally gets back together.

If you can find a way to snag those precious moments apart, do it! Be creative and flexible with when and how you get them. Enlist the help of your husband, close relatives, friends, older children, or other homeschooling parents. And remember, its not just for your sanity, it's for your kids sanity as well.

We shouldn't feel guilty for needing time away, for more reasons than I can list here. But I'll give you a few to help relieve your guilt and separation anxiety.

### Independence

Sometimes homeschooling parents don't quite know where that line is between helping our kids and needing to back off. Sometimes we're accused of not knowing when to cut those apron strings. It helps to remember that one of the purposes of homeschooling (and parenting, really) is to teach our kids to be independent of us.

It seems obvious, but we sometimes forget it: we won't always be here. Our children will grow up and, in most cases, move away. They will forge their own path and live their own lives. And even though you might forever be really important and they'll love you to squishy little pieces, you won't be the main character. And that's OK.

We have two responsibilities to our kids: to give them roots and to give them wings. As homeschoolers we go a great job at giving them good, deep roots. But we have to work on developing their strong healthy wings as well.

**Sibling Rivalry**

Siblings need time apart from siblings, plain and simple. I'm probably hyper sensitive to this seeing as how my kids are just over 12 months apart and, up until a year ago, shared a bedroom. But taking a step back, I see my kids wake up together, eat breakfast together, do chores together, do school together, play together, everything together. And while that's really charming when they get along, it's like nails on a chalkboard when they don't.

When siblings have the chance to untangle themselves from the mass that is Us, they have more breathing room to explore who they are. To find out what their interests and dislikes are. It's really important that your kids know they are Son and Daughter, not sonanddaughter. Make an effort to give your children time to explore who they are on their own.

## Learning from others

It is perfectly fine and necessary for your kids to know there are other people in the world they can learn and explore and experience with, not just mom and dad. Sometimes as homeschooling parents, because we aren't utilizing the public school system, we forget about the importance of our children learning from other people.

In the past year especially, we've concentrated on the boys learning from others. Branching out from our house and taking advantage of other learning experiences in the area. Everyone can teach our kids something and we've been delighted in the things we've seen happen.

But here's something you might not be aware of: your kids are completely different characters when they aren't around you. And they can do amazing things without your assistance or supervision.

My eldest was asked to serve breakfast for a benefit through Boy Scouts. Seeing as how my oldest traditionally won't say boo to anyone who doesn't share his address, I was quite interested to see how it would go. We showed up and he was instructed by his den leader as to how he could help: asking guests what they would like to drink and carrying the drinks to their table for them.

I was pretty sure it would be disaster. His tongue would dry up and fall off and he'd run out screaming when anyone said hello to him. I just knew it.

But you know what?

He was fine.

In fact he was more than fine. He was brilliant! I watched like a fly on the wall while he joked with people he didn't know, cleaned up people's messes (without being asked!) and ran his tail off helping everyone he could.

Who *was* this kid?

He'd come into his element. He'd stepped up the plate. And I honestly believe it had a lot to do with the fact that *I* wasn't in charge of the deal and *I* wasn't the one directing him.

And you know what? I refuse to be offended by that. And you shouldn't be, either.

Kids need to learn from other people. Kids need to be in situations where they take direction from other people. Out there in the big bad world, our kids will encounter so many things. We need to make sure we aren't unintentionally creating such a cushy and cozy life for them within homeschooling that we'll send them out into the world ill-prepared and lacking the knowledge of how things really work.

Sometimes our kids learn certain things best from other people.

Yes, parents are great teachers. Yes, teacher-parents have a vested interest in their student-children. But sometimes teacher-parents can't separate themselves as much as is healthy to do in certain situations.

Sometimes our kids need other people. And very often, so do we.

Other people give us all a break.

And so, you see, we shouldn't feel guilty when we need some time to ourselves. If it helps you, consider thinking of homeschooling as your job. You'll never get a paid lunch, but it's still very important that you take breaks to collect your thoughts. To breathe. To rejuvenate. To think about something other than how to get your kids to understand double digit multiplication. Occasional absence makes the heart grow fonder, and fondness surely makes a homeschooling parent's day easier.

# Chapter 3

## Unavoidable Potholes: Doubt and Guilt

It's wonderful to be in charge of your own path, isn't it? Homeschooling allows you a certain amount of freedom (and ironically, at the same time, control) in your educational life. We're in charge of the path and the decisions we have to make (or not make) are endless. How great is that?

It's awesome. Unless you think about it too much.

*Because* you are in charge of the path, there is so much to decide. And because there is so much to decide, there are so many opportunities to second guess yourself.

Will I cover it all? Am I doing too much?

Are they behind? Ahead? Why do I care?

Should I have more rules? Less?

I really try not to worry about my children's education. I want to be confident with the decisions we've made, the choices we've committed to. I don't want to wallow in the doubt and guilt of every possible *what if.* Because if you think about it too much, there's a lot of them.

But I'm human. And there are a heck of a lot of blogs, books, and speakers out there to give their opinion on how I'm doing.

Talking to other homeschoolers can sometimes be a supportive and encouraging experience. Other times, in the wrong frame of mind, it can be an excuse to start worrying that your family's homeschooling life is not as adventurous/peaceful/stimulating/academic/fill in the blank as the next family's. I think we've probably all been in that frame of mind at one time or another, and we know it can rip at our confidence and stir us into a giant pot of worry.

Welcome to homeschooling, located at the intersections of doubt and guilt.

Ask any parent and they'll probably agree that guilt is part of the package when you sign on to raise children. And since homeschooling is somewhat an extension of parenting, it follows that guilt would enter this package as well. It's just that as a homeschooling parent, you have a thousand other different things to potentially feel guilt about.

### Guilt brought on by others

Doubt and guilt often crop up when comparing ourselves to others, and not necessarily even other homeschoolers. Some people have the uncanny ability to make us question every solid decision we've made. They can make us feel wrong for every perfect choice we took. We doubt ourselves because we compare ourselves and our kids to someone else and someone else's kids. And we need to stop. Know why?

First off, it goes against the basis of homeschooling. Although there are as many different reasons to homeschool as there are people reading this book, I think we can all agree that our reason had something to do with not agreeing with the public school's idea of normal. So why do we merge onto the Homeschooling Highway and spend all our time comparing our Minivan of Awesome to someone else's?

But there's another reason to stop aiming for the potholes of comparison: Because the comparisons are often completely unfair.

Very often, if not always, we compare our private life to someone else's public life. If you read about homeschooling, the blogger or author will often talk about the good days: the awesome field trip, the science project that changed the world, the peaceful getaway where the whole family drummed around a campfire. They don't often, if ever, talk about the disaster days when they didn't get anything accomplished because there was fighting and the dog died and the refrigerator exploded and the milk was bad and mom yelled because she just doesn't get why Sammy doesn't remember where to put the remainder in a long division problem.

But you know what? Everyone has those days.

Everyone.

We need to stop checking our outtakes against the next family's highlight reel! We need to remember that we chose homeschooling so we could go our own way, do our own thing, according to the needs of our family. We're doing our own thing, remember? That's why we are here!

You are not the family standing next to you. Your kids are not your neighbor's kids. Your kids are yours, and you need to know them. That is why you educate the way you do.

My youngest is so happy-go-lucky and up for anything, it sometimes makes my head spin. My oldest, on the other hand, wants things a certain way and is sky-high anxious if he doesn't know what's coming next...and what's coming after that.

These are my kids. And I have to figure out how to live a life of learning with *my* kids. As soon as I start comparing them to everyone else's kids and weighing our decisions against the ones everyone else has made, I end up with some skewed vision and expectation of what's normal. And at that point, I'm completely dishonoring who they are as kids and who we are as a family.

Refusing to drop a tire into the pothole of comparisons will help immensely with doubt and guilt.

## You Got Something to Prove?

Sometimes we hop into our Minivan of Awesome believing we're supposed to produce perfection.

Or wait. That's probably not you. You're not into this to produce perfection, because you don't believe in it. But as long as you are here, you *are* going to show Ms. So-And-So that you can do this thing. And the better your kids behave or can rattle off the Preamble to the Constitution, the better you'll look.

Ahem.

Maybe it's because your mother-in-law said homeschooling was stupid. Maybe your friend said you'd peter out and not last the semester. Maybe it's because your brother was nominated for Teacher of the Year and you're feeling like you've got something to prove. Whatever it is, you're on a mission.

Unfortunately, your kids are paying the price.

Our duty as a homeschooling parent is to nuture, love, explore and enjoy. It's to be in this life with our kids in this choice we've made. It's not about producing perfection with the intention that perfection will somehow prove that homeschooling works. That's not the point, and if we make it the point, we have to realize it is a huge burden for our kids to carry.

**Don't believe everything you read**

The joy of the internet is there is a ton of information at the click of a mouse or the swipe of a finger.

But that's also the bane of its existence.

It is possible to find support for any choice online. It's easy to find someone to support any way of life that you're feeling cozy with. However you believe is the best way to bring up a child, you generally find a monster list of websites, forums, blogs, and groups out there to cheer you on in the life you're attempting to lead.

But be careful.

Hang on.

Because if you happen to rip across the wrong (right?) website, forum, blog, or group, you might find out that the same path you're currently on is bound to turn your darling children into maniacal criminals.

Amazing that something so wrong (right?) can be so right (wrong)!

Some people think homeschooling is the way, others think it's a passing fad. Even within homeschooling, people have conflicting views about which is the right way to proceed.

But that's all they are. Views. Opinions. Beliefs. They aren't fact. They aren't set in stone. And we have to remember that while we're driving along the road of homeschooling, there are people who are going to agree with us and there are people who are going to disagree. We are not required to change our mind because of anything they say or don't say. This isn't about them.

Repeat. Outloud. This is not about them.

It's all you, baby. (Or at least everyone in *your* Minivan of Awesome.)

## What if I'm totally screwing up the kids?

Once upon a time, on a long day when the coffee pot was on the fritz, I might have dramatically flopped onto my bed in a sea of tears exclaiming to my husband "How do you know we're not totally screwing up our children by homeschooling them?"

My husband, never one to mince words, asked "Do our kids *look* screwed up?"

I knew what he meant, but the hilarious thing (and what broke through the drama of my outburst) was that at that exact moment as I was supposed to be assessing whether or not my kids looked screwed up, my eldest walked by with every single article of clothing on inside out and backwards...with no shoes.

I burst out laughing.

I think as homeschoolers we sometimes worry about whether we've made the best choice for our kids, and sometimes that goes so far as to worry if we've possibly done worse than if we would have just followed the mainstream path. But really, if you take a look at your kids (the inside out, backwards, barefooted beauties that they are), ask yourself: do they seem screwed up? Are they healthy? Happy? Do they love learning? Is your life amazing?

Most likely, a resounding yes.

So learn to let it go. You are not screwing up your kids. You are giving them an amazing life of learning and choices and freedom and family.

That is not, and I repeat not, screwing up your kids.

Guilt, doubt and worry are not exclusive to homeschoolers. Any parent who cares for their children is apt to second guess their choices and worry if they've made the wrong one. There's always something to wonder about, and if we don't question ourselves about this thing, we'll question ourselves about another. The trick is not so get so caught up in the guilt, doubt and worry that it wrecks all the amazing things we're trying to do with our kids. You chose this life for a reason. If the giant semis of guilt and doubt and worry are holding you back, put your blinker on, pass them, and speed ahead! Your Minivan of Awesome doesn't need them. You've got a million more important things to deal with. Spend your time looking at scenery that makes your van full of folks smile, because that's what helps you the most on this curvy road of homeschooling.

# Chapter 4

## The Meeting of the Minivans:

## A Question of Socialization

My phone blinked with a message.

"Sorry I missed you," I said, returning my cousin's call. "The boys have some friends over and we were outside."

There was silence.

"Sorry," she finally said, with a very poor attempt to stifle a giggle.

"What's so funny?"

"Well...it's just that...your boys actually have *friends*?"

"Why wouldn't they?"

"I don't know," she said. "How would *your* boys actually meet other kids?"

Oh yeah, that's right. Because they're homeschooled.

Real conversation. Not even kidding.

I remember when we first merged onto the Homeschooling Highway. We got plenty of questions regarding how our children would make friends. How would we ensure they knew how to carry on a conversation with others? How would we know they could survive in a social situation without drooling and walking as if they had two left feet?

If you've been in the homeschooling world for longer than ten minutes, you know what a tired topic this is. Once you connect yourself with a local homeschooling community, a whole world of social activity opens up to you. It's almost obscene how many opportunities are available. Every hour, of every day. In fact, there are so many categorically *social* things to experience, you could homeschool and literally never have time to be home.

I remember the beginning of our homeschooling journey and how my mom would sometimes join us for the things we did. Sometimes it was a history field trip with our homeschool group. Other times it was an activity day like Gym Jam at the local community center. It didn't take her long to realize just how many opportunities were available to us and how very *many* people were partaking in those things.

"It's like once you get into it," I remember her saying, "A whole underground world reveals itself to you."

True that.

But the majority of folks who aren't on the road of homeschooling *don't* know that. And so we give a polite chuckle to their questions while we run our kids to their next social adventure. Don't you wish we could show them a day in the life?

Yep, the usual socialization conversation is pretty much the same old boring thing that stems from the fact that if you're not driving underground in a Minivan of Awesome, you simply haven't been exposed to our ridiculous world. But we have to make sure we don't completely turn off the subject of socialization. There are plenty of things we need to be aware of, admit, and own up to when it comes to the topic of getting our kids out there.

### It's more work for the parents

No, I don't believe children need to be in a class with 30 other kids their own age in order to learn social skills and form friendships.

But, let's be honest, shall we?

If you're in a class with 30 other kids, it's a heck of a lot easier.

If you're going to homeschool and *you* don't give your kids opportunities to meet and greet, they *can't* meet and greet (especially if they are younger).

I know. I just talked about the billion opportunities that are out there. But what I'm saying is that if *you* don't step up and put those opportunities on the calendar, your kids aren't going to be involved with them.

See the emphasis on the word you? It's up to you. Especially if your kids aren't driving. Especially if you live rurally where the nearest neighbor is three miles away and the nearest homeschooler is in the next town west.

It's up to you.

So many times people get into homeschooling and believe that the socializing is just going to happen. Just naturally. Just because kids breathe and have a pulse. (I can say that because I used to be one of those homeschoolers.) I thought *here we are on this fabulously free road of homeschooling, look at all those other cars...driving by...why aren't they stopping?*

Homeschooling parents have to put the work in to make it happen. If you don't, your kids don't reap the benefits. And neither do you.

Everyone's social needs are different. Every family finds comfort in different levels of social activity. But let's be honest. If you're an introverted parent (I'm raising my hand) and you were blessed with the biggest social butterfly known in the county (my youngest) you're going to have some explaining to do to your child who doesn't want to sit in the backyard weaving baskets anymore. Or you're going to have to bite the bullet, get out there, and be social.

*But we are social*, you cry. *My kids can talk to anyone! The cashier at the grocery store, the librarian, their 75 year old grandmother...*

Right. Okay. Let's talk about that.

## The difference between conversing and connecting

Some homeschooling parents will brag about how socially advanced their kids are because they can carry on a conversation with someone five times their age. And no doubt, it's quite admirable to be able to do that. But it's almost as if, because the public school glops kids together in nine month segments, some homeschoolers go out of their way to make sure their kids socialize completely *outside* of those parameters.

Sometimes at a detriment to their children.

We don't like to talk about things like this because we don't want to give any credit to the naysayers who would so love any bit of ammunition to blow up our way of life. But we can't deny there are homeschooling parents who are doing a less than awesome job of getting their kids "out there". If your son's entire social experience revolves around girls who are five years younger than him, how awesome is that? Sure, he's going to be great at understanding girls...but can we all agree that he might want a buddy who can pee standing up?

As a homeschooling parent, you have to work a little harder at providing those opportunities. It is not as easy as putting them on the bus every morning and knowing they are going to come in contact with who knows how many people before they return home. It is *your* job (and time and gas money) to make sure they are getting out of the house and seeing other living breathing humans they aren't related to.

But you're doing that, right?

Well...

There is a huge difference between giving our children opportunities to get out and talk to people, and giving our children opportunities to *connect* with people. It's wonderful if my nine-year-old can carry on a completely normal conversation with the 40-year-old at the deli.

That's being able to talk to people.

But is he going to call the 40 year old at the deli when he needs a tip on Skylanders or wants to have a birthday party? Probably not.

And that refers to connection.

We can talk all day about the definition of a friend and how we don't need to only be friends with people who are our age. But there is something to be said with taking that idea so far that our children have no connection with anyone remotely near their age. Homeschoolers sometimes have a fascination with extremes. Some believe that children "socialized" in the public school setting (ie, children very near their own age) are unable to talk to anyone outside their age group, so these homeschoolers spend their time making sure their kids can talk to everyone outside their age group...and forget the ones that are within it.

It's admirable to be able to talk with people of any age but we have to remember that connection is at least as, if not more, important. Does your child want to be able to ask the barista their opinion on coffee beans, or would your child rather know they've got friends they can call for comfort when their dog dies?

## Are you choosing their friends?

We all get tired of the normal socialization questions.

"What about birthday parties?"

"What about prom?"

If someone wants to argue homeschooling socialization with me, I at least want to hear an original question to bring me out of my heard-this-a-billion-times stupor.

"Don't most homeschooled kids only get to hang out with the kids of parents who are mutual friends?"

Aha. A new one.

And one I actually had to think about.

My children have a pretty varied group of friends. But, as I think more on it, the children that mine hang out with most are the children of parents I actually like spending time with.

In a public school classroom of 30 kids, a child is exposed to all sorts of personalities. Friendships may be formed between children whose parents might never speak to each other in their own social arena.

In homeschooling, that's not how it works. Until the kids can drive (or are involved in drop-off activities) it's a parent-controlled world. If a child is involved in something where participating parents blend like oil and water, the child probably won't be involved in that something for very long.

Social steering of the Minivan of Awesome is one of the benefits...and downfalls...of homeschooling, and something we need to keep in mind. Yes, as homeschoolers, we have more options for socially maneuvering our kids. And let's be honest – sometimes it's necessary. But are we turning them from a certain someone because we don't like their behavior...or because we can't stand to be in a room with their mom for more than two hours?

## Homeschooled children = well-mannered?

I often hear people rave about how well-mannered homeschooled children are.

And while this is sometimes true, we have to remember that kids are still kids and can do some pretty "amazing" things when you least expect it, regardless of who is teaching them to read and write. Homeschooled children are still quite capable of not wanting to get out of bed, declaring school stupid, mouthing off, and being a pest in public.

I'm sure it's not just my kids.

At least that's what I'm sticking with.

Homeschooling is not a cure-all for behavior. It gives you ample opportunities to monitor conduct and fix issues, but it isn't a bubble of protection. Homeschooling does not guarantee you will get away from hyper-spastic, terribly behaved kids *or* bullies. Kids run ridiculously out of control in both public school and homeschool. You'll still deal with rogue children; the ones who steal your Pokemon cards, break the castle you built, or ruin your science experiment. You will probably, however, have slightly more control over how you deal with the situation and the people involved.

We forget that some people choose homeschooling *because* of their children's behavioral issues! They don't feel their public school system can deal with their child's issues properly, so they keep them home for education. The child running through the halls at the science museum's homeschool days might have been pulled from school because his mother wanted to personally deal with his tendency to throw chairs at his classmates.

Polite and well-mannered? Not necessarily.

## Social needs change

In public school, children get together to learn. (And I know some of us will have to use that term loosely because we all have our own opinions about public school.) In homeschooling, a good chunk of the lessons are done at home, and the "getting together" is mostly in an effort to hang out or socialize. (Again, we'll probably have to use that description loosely because we all have our own opinions about how much learning happens during socialization.) In homeschooling we have the Almighty Social Group, made up of people who school the same way or live in the same area or are somehow similarly grouped together. We find one that fits, join up, and relax into a forever friendship with everyone involved.

Right?

Well, it could be...if Life and Children never changed

There's a shift that occurs at some point where a child really starts to dive into their own interests. Their personality shines through and they become Who They Are Going to Be. And while that's all wonderful and fine, occasionally it throws a giant wrench into things. Sometimes there is a glitch between what they've always done and what they want to do now. Sometimes they struggle with the realization that who they've always hung out with is not who they want to hang out with now.

Think about your own childhood. Remember back to the end of 4th grade? Remember the friends that were going to be your friends forever? (And ever?) And you went through the three months of summer...and something changed. You arrived at the first day of 5th grade and suddenly those forever friends...well, things were just different. You'd changed. You didn't have the same things in common anymore. Your interests were different. You were growing and figuring yourselves out. And you just didn't click anymore. So you entered 5th grade, you found new friends in the giant pool of kids who were in school with you...and you moved on.

In homeschooling, that's not so easy.

A friend of mine (who has been homeschooling ages longer than I) remembers the time her daughter hit the Brick Wall of Change.

"It's not that I don't want to be friends with them anymore," her daughter sobbed. "But what we do when we are together is boring! I don't want to do what they want to do. We have nothing in common to talk about!"

My friend and her daughter had been in the same homeschool group for five years. Her daughter had always enjoyed going and seemed to be friends with everyone there. But the year she turned 11, things were different. When the group started, the kids had spanned the ages of 3-9. Five years later, those same kids made up a group of 8-15 year olds...which made for a completely different ballgame.

"When my daughter first struggled with this," my friend told me, "I wanted her to work through it. I told her I understood that people were growing up and changing. People's opinions and interests were different. But I wanted her to know it was perfectly acceptable to hang out with others who don't see eye to eye or who aren't necessarily our best friend in the entire world. They'd lost some common ground, but I really thought things would be ok."

They weren't.

A few months went by. My friend said she could tell her daughter was putting in the effort of really trying to find some common ground, but it wasn't working anymore.

"The kids were just simply changing," my friend admitted. "You know, when a group starts and five-year-old boys are running around with eight-year-old girls...that's completely different than when those same boys are ten and those girls are thirteen. It's a different world. My daughter had reached a place where she needed something different. And I had to realize that was ok."

Kids growing up and growing apart is a completely natural part of life. We can't fault kids for doing it. Sometime in the future (if it hasn't already happened on your journey so far) you might be forced to look at the situation realistically and say Look, Self. This is the pool of kids my kids are picking their buddies from. This is the pool of kids I want my kids to get close with and form long lasting connected relationships with. Are my kids feeling that anymore with this group? Do they have anything in common with them anymore?

Maybe not. Maybe it's time to move on.

Problem is, it's really hard to deal with that. Kids *and* adults agreed.

Homeschooling groups are almost always smaller and more connected. The friendships extend farther than just the kids; the parents end up becoming friends as well. The boundaries around acceptable group behavior in homeschooling are (in my experience) much larger than with a group of kids/families in a public school setting. Therefore, when things happen or change in the homeschooling group, the effects are much different than if the same thing would have happened in a group ten times its size. In a public school, there are more people to bounce off of. More people to soften the blow. In homeschooling, we just don't have that same buffer. And yes, it's a valuable learning experience and we have to figure out how to deal with some issues that larger groups would just ignore and move on from, but figuring out how to deal involves work and emotions and a parent that is willing to handle the very real and very big feelings that come out of growing up and growing apart.

Regardless of where your child is schooled, some friendships will continue on, and some will be left behind. Some will just become more casual. Our job as homeschooling parents is to make sure we are giving our children options of flexibility to deal with the growing up and growing apart that is a natural part of childhood.

In speaking with veteran homeschoolers, they've stressed the importance in making sure that children's social needs are met (especially as the kids get older). And not in the way that we need to worry about prom or birthday parties, because I really think those are the least of our worries. Socializing is different as children age. When your kids are 5 and 6, they are socializing by playing. It's a play date. When your kids are 12 and 13, the social aspect of homeschooling is completely different. And we know that in our head...I think...but we can't seem to get our heads around it when our kids are asking for something different than what we've all been so comfortable with in the forever leading up to this point.

Let's hear it for socialization, right?

Sigh.

Socialization as a homeschooler really doesn't have anything to do with what people often ask us about. As far as

I know, none of us in the Minivan of Awesome are worried about our kids drooling and tripping over their feet while they are out in the world, as so many people "out there" seemed to be concerned with. Even so, we can't completely ignore the subject of socialization. Merging onto the Homeschooling Highway makes us, by nature, a bit unique. So it only makes sense we get our own unique socialization issues to deal with!

# Chapter 5

## In Charge of the Car:

## Your Responsibility as a Homeschooling Parent

The actual mission of the Minivan of Awesome depends a bit on your original reasons for choosing to homeschool. Maybe you want freedom. Maybe you want a challenge. Maybe you want to rearrange the walls that have been placed around each child so they can find their way out to bigger and better things. Perhaps you want to open your children up to the vast number of possibilities that await them in whatever means you can.

Maybe you just want to survive math.

Our purpose is to work ourselves out of a job. We teach our kids so they can become independent of us. We want to bring our children up as fully functioning, responsible adults.

There are so many things we want to do with homeschooling and so many ways to make those things happen. But I think the success of the journey boils down to a few very important things, one of them being top on the list: You.

Yes, you. Your involvement. Your provisions, be it time, money, chauffeuring, or something else. If you're going to homeschool, you have to be involved.

But we know that, right? We're the parents who get accused of being hyper-involved in our kids' lives. We know all about involvement.

Believe me, for every homeschooling parent out there doing this, that, and the other thing together with their kids, there's another parent out there who is significantly less involved. Maybe even completely hands off. And not because their kid is requesting it.

You signed up for this gig. You.

Now I'm not saying you have to dump a billion dollars a year into your child's educational experience. And I'm not requiring that you set off for a 23-hour-a-day sightseeing excursion across the country. But what I am saying is that if you decide to homeschool and you as the parent slack off, you are not giving your child the educational and life experience that was intended with your original decision to homeschool.

I've met parents who freely admit they chose to homeschool simply because they wanted to be home. Now, I'm not sure if they saw the billboard, but *being home* and *homeschooling* are two completely different things. Choosing to homeschool is making a commitment to your children and their learning.

Notice I didn't say schooling.

If you're a curriculum lovin' homeschooler, but you slack on all your lessons because your brain is somewhere else 99% of the day, you may need to reconsider what your intentions with homeschooling were.

If you're in the unschooling frame of mind, but tell your kids they can't explore this or that or something else because you don't have time for it (read: you're signed up to volunteer for fourteen other things that don't even involve your kids), you might want to take a look at what your homeschooling intentions were.

If you choose to homeschool because you want to open the world up to your kids, but then immediately shut the world down...what really was your point in homeschooling? I know gas is expensive. I know it takes time to run kids here and there. I know your own backyard is a rich environment of learning. But if your kid wants to learn fiddle or robotics or advanced chemistry or soccer or theater lighting design, and you can't provide that, you have two options: you say no, over and over and over again...or you bite the bullet and get them involved in the places they can learn those things.

If we *choose* to homeschool and then spend all our time complaining that we have no time for ourselves, we need to take a look at our true intentions. You do realize you agreed to keep your kids home with you, right? Home. Where you live. With you. Yes, a homeschooling parent needs a break, but *getting a break* is different than constantly complaining that you've lost yourself. If you're staring blankly at your children and wondering *who are these kids and why do they keep bothering me* it's worth taking a deeper look at other educational options.

If you choose to homeschool, homeschooling has to be the priority.

Yes, I know that homeschooling fits nicely into life and that you very often can't separate the two from each other. Some people can't wrap their heads around making homeschooling a priority because it would be like asking someone to remember to breathe. Some people simply don't need to be reminded. But others get sucked in by the realization that when you homeschool, not only do the kids have more free time, the adults do, too. And suddenly everyone is filling up their free time with everything that has nothing to do with anyone else. Unfortunately, that free time starts spilling into the time everyone was supposed to be working on this Homeschooling Thing. A family might start out the journey in one Minivan of Awesome, and eventually everyone has defected to their own Mini Countries of

Isolation. And while that might work for awhile, sometimes it's hard to rally the troops back together.

Now don't feel bad. I'm lecturing here out of honesty because there was a time and place (and even occasionally still) where I had to remind myself that I chose to stay home and homeschool. As an introverted writer, I immensely enjoy the time I get to work on my stuff. And I fell into the trap of "If I could just eke out a little more time for my writing...if we could just plow through math a little quicker..." A stern talking was given to me, however, that pointed out something huge. Some people thought I'd chosen to homeschool simply so I could have the excuse to stay home and write. But for my husband and I, the option had always been offered for me to stay home and write and send the kids to public school.

But I chose to keep them home.

I chose to take responsibility for their education.

So my decisions have to be based upon *that*.

My kids will not always be here, and neither will yours. Ask anyone who has homeschooled a child through graduation and they will tell you, looking back, the time went Just. Like. That. Do we want to look back and feel guilty because we had our attention on three hundred other things, or didn't give as much as we know we could have?

Homeschooling is not something we have to do, it is something we *get* to do.

## A gentle nudge

My oldest would rather be at home. Given the choice to go *someplace* and be involved in *something*, he would always err on the side of crawling in a cave, feigning unconsciousness. And while I respect the fact he prefers the comforts of home, it's not healthy to always be at home.

And besides. Spending the majority of our time holed up at home was not the reason we chose to homeschool. The point was to make our children's world bigger, not smaller.

So when my painfully introverted oldest told me again he had no desire to do anything outside of home, my response to him was a community education flyer and the task of finding one thing – anything – to sign up for.

He chose football, but wasn't happy about it. And the night before his first class he sobbed in his bunk, telling me a thousand different things that could go wrong with the whole experience.

But you know what?

Once his class started, he loved it.

It's been this way with many things. Scouts, Lego Robotics class, chemistry camp, meeting the neighbor kid, you name it. He doesn't want to do it because it's something new. But then his mean ol' mom makes him try, and...he loves it.

A loving and gentle nudge is perfectly ok.

Even if our kids say they aren't interested.

"I'm not interested" used to be tossed around a lot at the beginning of our journey. And if our kids said they weren't interested we listened to them and didn't pry.

But I caught on to them.

Sometimes "I'm not interested" means "is this going to interrupt my time to play Wii?" Sometimes it means "my friend tried that and said it was dumb so I think it is dumb, too." Sometimes it means "I don't care what this activity is, if there will be more than four people there, I'm not going." Sometimes it means "it starts at nine in the morning? Are you nuts?"

I think we run a huge risk as homeschoolers when we fall into the "he's not interested" trap. We want so much for our children to explore their interests that we cave to them being *un*interested in something. But let me ask, how wordly is a nine year old – yes, even an ultra-mature homeschooler? They can't possibly know everything that's out there. At 33 years old, I sure don't! So occasionally mom and/or dad have to gently nudge them in certain directions with a "try it, you might like it".

This might take money. This might mean you driving somewhere and sitting for two hours, bored out of your mind. This might mean plastering a smile on your face while he struggles because you know in your gut once he gets there he will love it.

Remember, you signed up for this gig. And gentle nudges are part of the gig.

We have to remember we've been on the planet longer than our kids. We know of things that exist that aren't even on their radar yet. So if we don't expose our child to karate or dance or sculpting or WWII or the history museum or welding or animal husbandry...who will?

The public school?

Oh, that's right. Our kids *aren't there.*

Public school sometimes gets a bad rap for exposing kids to a ton of different topics but never giving time for in depth exploration. And while there are definite disadvantages to learning everything that way, it's not completely bad. Some homeschools are known for exposing their kids to a few things in depth, and forget about allowing time to experience a ton of different things.

Can we find the happy medium somewhere in our Minivan of Awesome?

**Let me entertain you...**

One advantage of homeschooling is you can get done in three hours what it takes the public school eight.

Turns out, that can also be a disadvantage.

Independence is valued in many homeschools. We all want people to be impressed with how early our children can make their own lunch or do their own laundry. My, aren't they helpful?

But there is a huge difference between how young a child can make their own peanut butter sandwich, and how young a child can entertain herself, undirected, for a significant amount of time.

As has already been well established, I'm an introvert. I need time to myself in order to survive. So after three hands-on hours with the kids on whatever I'm teaching them that day, I need some time to decompress. Not to mention time to feed the animals, do the laundry and make supper.

It's not as if I'm doing anything they can't be involved in. I don't disassociate myself from my kids for the rest of the day. But the kids aren't necessarily being directed in any particular manner and are pretty much free to do what they want, short of setting off fireworks in the barn.

Or at least that's how we did it in the beginning. And it didn't last very long.

Within an hour of being done with school, they'd be running wildly inside the house or pounding each other into the ground. At first I would redirect, redirect, and redirect again, but it generally ended at me blowing up with "There are plenty of chores to do if you're that bored" or "we can have school longer if you can't handle the unstructured time…"

It wasn't long until a somewhat unpopular opinion washed over me.

Maybe children of a certain age can't handle that unstructured time.

Maybe they simply can't do it, and it's no fault of their own.

My children's publicly schooled counterparts were being told what to do and had responsibilities ten or more hours a day while in the big brick building. My children were *in school* for three.

That's a difference of seven hours, and it doesn't take some kids long to get bored.

And in the middle of yet another screaming match which ended with me blasting, "I'm not here to entertain you!" it occurred to me that in fact, maybe I was.

Who signed up for this gig again?

Oh. Yeah. That's right.

Some people are really good at filling their time, others not so much. Some are content to stare out the window at the scenery going by, while others collapse into insanity without a list of things on how to pass the time. That adult you see freaking out in line at the DMV because it's moving slow, he's bored and (oh gosh) has a dead iPhone? That's my kid, minus twenty years, when he doesn't have something specific to do.

It has been argued that part of the reason that public school keeps the hours it does is because it a) gives the kids *something to do* and b) keeps the kids out of trouble so the parents can hold regular jobs.

Kids who get done with school in three hours have a lot of time to kill. And some kids are really good at killing time. Others, even with parents who provide plenty of things to do outside of school time, aren't the best at undirected activities.

A hundred years ago, this wasn't an issue. Families (parents and children) were so busy, if the kids were given an hour of free time, they had a billion ideas of how to fill it. Free time was rare.

It almost seems as if we've gone the other way. The direction we get in public school is many times unfulfilling busy work, and the shorter direction we get in homeschooling (if any) leaves for the majority of the day to be wide open for exploration....or trouble?

Think of it as an adult. You know how when you've got all day to get something done, you laze about and dawdle and get distracted and hungry and crabby and tired? But when you've only got a half hour to accomplish the same task, you get right to work?

Same thing. Giving the kids three hours of direction and allowing the rest of the time to "find their own fun" might, with some kids, end up with a lazing, dawdling, distracted, tired, crabby mess.

And the whole time you're thinking, "What!? I wanted you to be free to explore! Go explore!"

I've been blasted plenty for opinions like this. Some homeschoolers tell me that if I'd just strew enough fabulous materials around my five acre farm, the kids would never have to come to me for anything because they'd be so gleefully entertained with life. (By the way, more strewing = more work for the person who signed up to homeschool.) And while this might solve the issue for some kids in some families at some five acre farms, it simply doesn't help my boys. Kids are all different, right?

As time has passed, the boys have gotten significantly more skilled at self entertainment. Part of that is because they're getting older and are jumping into their own things and figuring out their own interests. But the other part is I've realized that what they're wanting isn't so much something to do as it is one-on-one interaction. When they fill up their tank with Mom's attention, they're much more ready to go. I had to learn that three hours of school in the morning and the rest of the day apart doesn't hold them. They had to learn Mom can't hold them all day.

And the way we dealt with that, class, is called compromise.

### You actually have to teach

It's no secret, and few people will argue, that homeschooling can be academically superior to public school. Test scores consistently show that homeschoolers knock the socks off their publicly schooled counterparts. Among parents of academically gifted children, they often state they didn't feel public school would be able to challenge their child as well as a parent could at home.

I guarantee you though, not all of these parents have brought their child home to challenge them. Or maybe they did, and got sucked into other theories along the way.

I know, because I was one of those parents.

When my oldest was two he was speaking in full sentences and asking questions like "why does bark stay on trees?" and "why do we need two eyes if we can see just fine out of one?" I remember bringing him to the doctor for a check up and watching the doctor's eyes grow wider...and wider...as my two year carried on a completely normal conversation with her.

"You realize how much he knows, right?" she asked, and I nodded. And I knew we were in for days ahead that would exhaust my brain.

We chose to homeschool.

And yet, with a beginning like that, I have to ask myself: am I challenging his brain as much as I thought the public school couldn't?

Hmmm.

I can honestly say that at first, we weren't. Slowly, we became aware of the hypocrisy of our choice. How could we badger the school about why they weren't challenging their smartest students (which led to boredom extraordinaire) and yet, we *were not* challenging *our* son. Yes, we were giving him freedom. Yes, he had a thousand billion books to read. Yes, he was always creating science experiments. But were we specifically challenging him...the majority of the original reason we'd decided to homeschool him?

Hmmmm.

### How do I look, Mom?

Homeschool parents are in a tricky spot. We want to do what works best for us, and yet we know everything we do is stacked up and measured by many non-homeschoolers. As if our children's ability to spell, multiply, and quote Shakespeare on demand to a stranger is some sort of comment on the validity of homeschooling everywhere.

We're not going to please everyone. It's impossible, in any vein of life. And yet, I've seen some homeschool parents who go out of their way to make sure the whole world knows their child doesn't follow society's norms or the scope and sequence that other kids follow.

You know. The ones who get all the press when someone wants to take a jab at the merits of homeschooling.

And hey, if that works for you, that's great. Remember, your choice is perfect. But we also need to consider how we appear to people who don't homeschool. It's your choice, of course, as to whether you *care* about it, but we still need to be *aware* of it. When our children are not with us, they need to be able to function in the real world. Because we have chosen to step away from the public school system and a big chunk of normal life, we will be under scrutiny from many different people.

When any child can't spell his last name, doesn't know his address, or can't multiply, it often reflects poorly upon his school. If you're a homeschooler, well...where does that leave you?

No, you don't necessarily have to care what someone else thinks about what you're doing. I realize as a homeschooler, it's probably in your genetic makeup not to. But you have to understand that you will run into people who have an opinion about what you're doing and how you're doing it. That's just the way it is.  And if you're the only homeschooler that person ever talks to, you've probably just cemented their general opinion about homeschooling  - whether that's for the good or the bad.

Oh, I know we homeschoolers have never done that. You know, met someone and based our opinion about the whole group on that one person. (Wait. I think there's a chapter here somewhere about labels...and homeschoolers not getting along...)

Never mind.

There's a giant gray area between not caring what people think...and giving homeschoolers a bad name. Come on – do you really want to discredit all the hard work those homeschoolin' mamas and papas are out there doing? Why do we have homeschoolers flaunting the fact their nine year old can't spell his last name and doesn't know his address because he's never away from home? Why do we have homeschoolers overzealously publicizing the fact that they do school in their pajamas everyday or don't wake up until after noon?

Come on. Really?

Everyone has a different way of running their homeschool. We've all got quirks. We need to learn the difference between doing what we do because it works for us, and doing what we do to draw attention to the fact that we do things differently. The difference, my friends, is huge!

As homeschooling parents, we're in charge of that Minivan of Awesome. Regardless of how much we let our children help steer, we're still the ones holding the license. That license comes with responsibilities. The most important thing to remember is that we are not required to have that license. We *chose* to have that license. So get out there and drive your Minivan of Awesome like you mean it!

## Chapter 6

## The Family Who Schools Together...

## Freaks Everyone Else Out

I clearly remember when my extended family got word that we planned to homeschool. It was Easter. We'd just moved to a new home and everyone wanted to know if our oldest was excited to start kindergarten in a new town.

"I'm not going to school," our five year old stated matter-of-factly. "Mom is going to teach me."

Oh.

My.

Goodness.

Is it hot in here?

Can someone pass the corn? Or the ham? Or the wine?

And then, the questions started.

"Your *mom* is going to teach you?"

"How does that work?"

"How will you know what to teach him?"

"Is it expensive?"

"I knew someone who was homeschooled once..."

"Aren't you worried about socialization?"

Ah, homeschooling. A lovely life where you get to be the odd one in the corner at Thanksgiving dinner because you made this weird decision that no one quite gets. You might get peculiar comments. Long stares. Strange questions. Nasty comments.

Ah, homeschooling.

It's no fun to feel like you're being doubted or insulted. And when you're in the Minivan of Awesome, it always seems as though there's someone in your family or circle of friends who wants to mess up your plans for peaceful travel.

Maybe you've come up against *Ms. I'm Going To Quiz Your Kids.*

Nothing messes with your head more than someone asking your children random trivia while they are sneaking their second piece of pumpkin pie. You realize that your children's hesitation before answering entirely disproves the effectiveness of homeschooling for Ms. I'm Going To Quiz Your Kids. She's over the top. She'll ask your kids who the 23rd President of the United States was and wait with her foot tapping for their response... even though none of the other adults in the room know the answer without consulting their iPhones.

(By the way, the answer is Benjamin Harrison).

Or maybe you've met *Miss I'm Going To Assume Everything You Do With Your Kids Means You Don't Think I'm Doing Enough With Mine.*

She's pretty nutty, too. And insecure. She seriously thinks I spend nights awake thinking of all the different ways I can make her feel like a total jerk because she doesn't stay home to teach her kids. Don't you know the entire reason my family went to the Science Museum was so that we could talk about it at Thanksgiving and make all the non-homeschoolers feel like losers?

My favorite naysayer has to be *Mr. What Makes You Think You Can Teach Your Kids?*

I get the giggles every time I see him. He has this totally believable way of asking me (with a completely straight face) how I can teach second grade "stuff". He cracks me up! He almost makes me forget that his asking how I think I can teach second grade math means he's insinuating I can't *do* second grade math!

How in the world does one seriously deal with the constant questions, without reverting to the obvious sarcasm in the examples above?

Homeschoolers getting along with non-homeschoolers has everything to do with a whole heap of patience and a little sprinkle of education.

In my experience, there are two main reasons that non-homeschoolers might make questionably nasty comments to their homeschooling counterparts.

**Possible reason number one: they feel threatened and/or judged.**

You homeschool and they don't.

Simple enough statement, right?

Not exactly. Some people read into that as "You homeschool and you think I'm a bad parent because *I don't*." It's a bit like being around a vegetarian while chomping down a cheeseburger. It can be a bit convicting.

A friend of mine named Patty was (as many of us are) the only homeschooler in her extended family. She found get-togethers with her relatives to be strained, to say the least. The subject of school seemed to put everyone in an awkward position. With so many cousins running around, the way Patty's family chose to deal with The Homeschool Thing (as they called it) was simply to not talk about school at all. Now that would seem to be a simple, well intentioned solution, but the problem is that homeschoolers often don't draw a line between school and life. One is the same as the other. When someone asked Patty's kids "So what have you been up to?" they were probably going to hear about the fabulous science experiment they had growing in the refrigerator or the field trip they went on with co-op or the patio furniture they were learning to weld...or...or...or. But they couldn't talk about that, because even though it was their life...it also fell under that Homeschool Thing They Did.

So because Patty's extended family had made school discussions off limits, they had effectively (without knowing it) shut down her kids' conversations about life in general. We wouldn't want a simple conversation starter about the sudden change in weather to have Patty's kids bring up a recent field trip to the Museum of Meterology, would we?

Oh, the horror!

Patty was livid. It wasn't fair that aunts and uncles were ignoring her children simply because a discussion about the kids' day might bring up something homeschoolish and make the other public-schoolish kids and parents feel...bad? Left out? Uncomfortable?

"Do they actually think I'm sitting in judgment of everything their kids do or don't do in public school?" Patty asked me.

Patty, I think you've hit on something.

My friend made the decision to sit her extended family down and set the record straight.

"Look," she said. "I'm not here to tell you how to raise your kids. My decision to homeschool has *nothing to do* with your decision not to."

That really changed things between Patty and her extended family. Very often people aren't so much criticizing your choice to do something as they just want to know you aren't criticizing their choice *not* to do the same thing. As soon as Patty made it clear that she wasn't sitting and taking notes on what terrible parents they all were, somehow the conversations flowed more freely.

And her sons even got to talk about random science experiments and field trips.

Some people just have a knack for taking things personally. Sometimes it doesn't matter what you say, you know the other person is itching to stir up the waters and bring a giant tsunami of total destruction upon you and your non-public schooling family.

"So you decided to homeschool?" they might ask, and you immediately take on a deer in the headlights stance.

"Why," they continue, "would you want to do that?"

Sometimes you know it isn't going to matter what you say. It's not going to be good. They are going to start a fight.

You: We didn't like the public school.

Them: My kids go there. Are you saying I'm a bad parent?

You: I didn't want my child to be bored in public school.

Them: My kid is there. Are you saying she's not as smart as yours?

You: I wanted to spend more time with my kids.

Them: Are you saying I don't want to be with mine?

Like I said, sometimes it doesn't matter. Perhaps the best answer could be "Actually, we chose to homeschool because I just wanted to see what I could do to make the relatives get all up in arms and question their own worth as a parent by assuming I am making a comment on their child rearing skills and parental devotion. It looks like I chose the right thing to do!"

That might shut everyone up.

Maybe.

Can you imagine if every topic at a family gathering was so weighted?

Them: So what did you have for breakfast this morning?

You: Cheerios.

Them: Are you saying that because I fed my family eggs, I'm trying to poison them with cholesterol?

Or...

Them: I hear you bought a new car!

You: Yep, a Chevy.

Them: I suppose you think because we bought a Toyota we're not supporting the American-made economy.

See how ridiculous it sounds?

Part of the reason some people get a bit snarky about homeschooling or not homeschooling is that it brings out the Mama Bear factor. The one that says *my children, family and the choices I've made about them are being attacked. It's time to bring out the claws and fangs.* We see Mama Bear come out with co-sleeping (or not). Attachment parenting (or not). Breastfeeding (or not). Vaccinations (or not). We're competitive. We want the best for our kids. If someone insinuates we're failing them, our hair bristles and we stand up for the choices we spent so much time poring over...no matter which side of the fence we're standing on.

The problem is that all these people feeling threatened or judged makes communication flat out impossible.

### Possible reason number two: they don't understand it.

It's hard for us to believe, but not everyone *gets* homeschooling. Since homeschooling is our day-to-day normal, we forget it isn't even *on* some people's radar.

That is until they show up at Christmas and someone's kids are talking about incubating duck eggs in their kitchen for "school".

Case in point: Dedra, who told me it looked like I was having so much fun homeschooling my kids...maybe when her toddlers grew up, I could just homeschool them, too.

I chuckled and told her that wasn't an option.

"Why not?" she asked.

"Well, it's not allowed in our state."

"Oh, come on. How would the state even know?" she said.

"The superintendent sure would when you sent in your paperwork," I said.

She looked at me funny.

"The superintendent knows you homeschool?"

"I sure hope so, since that's where all our annual paperwork and report cards go."

Her face screwed up and she sighed.

"Gosh, I guess I didn't realize homeschooling was so technical."

I informed her of all the legalities (which completely depend on which state you're homeschooling in and how many times they change the requirements).

"I guess I had it wrong. I guess I thought you just revolved your day around field trips and a couple math problems."

Occasionally, yes. But most times it's a whole heck of a lot more involved.

Case in point: Theodore, who said to me, "Let me get this straight. You wake up in the morning and decide it would be a good day to talk about...apples...so you say a couple things about apples and call that school?"

Real conversation. Not kidding.

When people make blatantly rude comments about homeschooling, you're faced head-on with the decision of how to respond. Snotty sarcasm? Silence?

"I mean," he continued. "How do you even know where your kid is supposed to be educationally and what you're supposed to teach him when? You can't talk about apples forever."

In this instance (and most, to tell the truth) I chose to be the bigger person and educate Theodore. I let him know that there are plenty of places (like a scope and sequence) that will suggest what to teach a kid when. There are gazillion different curriculums available to buy. There are annual norm-referenced tests.

"You have to test your kids?"

"Required by the state of Minnesota, once a year."

With that, his entire demeanor changed.

"Oh!" he said. "Well, I guess I just thought..."

Yeah. I know what you thought. That I just pull something out of the air to teach my kids for a few minutes and we spend the rest of the day watching Spongebob in our pajamas. I get it.

Homeschoolers often forget (because we're in this underground subculture everyday) that not everyone knows what we do. In fact, hardly anyone does. Homeschooling isn't mainstream. And if the only exposure the mainstream society has to homeschooling is extremely biased news stories about the most radical unschoolers, it makes sense that most people we encounter won't have a clue about what we do on a daily basis. When people don't understand something, they either ask to have it explained, or they make their own assumptions.

Most people err on the side of assumption.

Theodore later told me he didn't initially understand what homeschooling was. He had an idea of what it entailed, but admitted that idea was totally wrong. He thanked me for educating him and keeping a pleasant attitude.

Which brings me to my next point.


**Homeschoolers can sometimes be scary to talk to.**


If you stick your neck out to choose a lifestyle outside the norm, you can be assured not everyone will understand or like what you do.

Those in the Minivan of Awesome have to deal with this a lot.

However.

When talking about non-homeschooling family members and friends being defensive, sensitive, or easily offended, it's only fair that we own up to the fact that we homeschoolers can be just as defensive, sensitive, or easily offended.

Oh. You don't think so?

We're defensive when the cashier at the grocery store asks our kids if they are excited to start school in September. *What makes them assume our kids are in school? Why does everyone always assume that public school is the only way? Why do they need to talk to my kids anyway?*

We're worried when the school district's number comes up on our caller ID. *Why are they calling? What do they want this time? Why are they so against me? I've got HSLDAs number ready to go...*

We're overly sensitive when someone innocently suggests our child sign up for a community education class to get out and see what's out there. *Are they suggesting I keep my kids locked in the basement? Don't they know my kids* are social butterflies and have friends in all corners of the country?

We're offended when someone recommends that our child might understand something better if taught differently. *Don't you think I know my own child? Being taught differently is the entire point of homeschooling, and I've bought the be-all, end-all of homeschooling curriculums!*

Okay. Not every homeschooler acts like that all the time. But, if we're honest, we might all have occasionally come close. I think we can all admit to knowing one or two homeschoolers who walk around half-cocked, looking for a reason to go off or start a fight. And a Minivan of Awesome that suffers from road rage is a dangerous thing.

In a previous homeschooling life, I might have been accused of being overly sensitive, defensive and easily offended. But I found myself in a situation that taught me just how much assuming we all do, and it really changed my mind.

One summer, my kids and I were out and about, and a female customer in a coffee shop took a shine to my espresso drinking young men. They started talking and, as always happens, the subject of school came up.

At the time, I remember wondering *Why does this woman assume my kids are in public school? Why can't people open up their minds a little? You know, if people would just...*

"We're homeschooled," my oldest answered, and I waited for the questions, comments, and concerns to fly.

But they didn't. Instead, the gal just took a sip of her tea, smiled at the boys, and said, "I homeschool my kids, too."

As human beings, we do a lot of assuming. And as human beings we want to be right. Those two things alone can get us in a ton of trouble, and the ability for homeschoolers and non-homeschoolers to communicate without cat claws can sometimes hinge on those two very human tendencies.

Sometimes our family get-togethers are all about the homeschooling because we *make it* all about the homeschooling. We're obnoxious about the fact we've made this choice. We get our jabs in wherever we can, and at the same time, put up walls that make it really hard for our family and friends to have any idea how to ask us something about homeschooling without us snapping their heads right off.

We can be hypocritical. We get mad that people don't ask us about our homeschooling life, but when they do, we are annoyed they are being so nosy.

Or we go over the top and say things like "We are not homeschoolers. We are home learners. We don't do school."

We listen to family and friends complain about being sad their children are going back to school at the end of summer, and we make completely insensitive remarks like "Well, that's why I homeschool. I don't have to send them away."

Now, come on. You know what that sounds like to someone who doesn't homeschool, right?

We need to stop. Yes we're driving the Minivan of Awesome, but some of us need to get over ourselves long enough to take a breath and respond to people in a way that casts homeschooling in a positive light. Do we want homeschooling to viewed by the mainstream as a viable option, or something that's been taken over by moody and out of control minivan drivers?

Remember Theodore? I set him straight, but did it nicely. There are many ways to explain ourselves without being nasty. We should be confident in our answers, but we don't have to be snotty or rude. We can answer the question kindly, even if we've been asked a hundred times. We can be warm. We can be polite. And it's not just about being nice for the sake of niceness.

It's because our kids are watching.

The way our children learn to deal with people is partially by watching us. We know that, but we forget that it means how we deal with people in all situations. Not just the bright sunshiny ones. How we deal with other people and their questions to us is really about what it's teaching our kids. This is real life learning for them! This is how our kids learn it's important to stand up for what your family believes in, and that there are really great ways (and really rotten ways) to go about that. This is how our children learn about civil conversation and choosing their battles. This is how our kids learn that even though we are comfortable with our decision, and that it is normal for us, it isn't necessarily so with other people.

If my son sees me getting snaggy with the cashier because they asked what is (more often than not) a simple conversation starter...what is he learning?

And what are we teaching the general public? That it is better to just not have a conversation with the kids in the checkout line because they might be homeschoolers and their mom might snap?

Not at all.

Let's please not be scary. Let's please not be unapproachable.

People who went through the public school system were raised believing that learning is taught and measured in a certain way. It's hard for them to wrap their heads around the many different ways we are figuring out how to do it. When Grandma or Uncle Jimmy or your best friend from high school asks what exactly this Homeschool Thing is, 4 ¾ times out of five, it's just because they care about your family and want to know what the heck is going on. Mostly, people just want to know that kids are learning something that will help them be a happy thriving member of society in the future. In the end, that's the goal, right? We just have different ways of getting there. It's our job to help our extended family and friends learn about those differences in a lovely warm way that keeps us approachable, them supportive, and the lines of communication open.

It takes time for extended family and friends to understand what homeschooling *is* and *is not*. My husband and I don't get a lot of flack anymore for our choice, and I like to think that's because people have seen what it is for us and that it works.

Either that, or after all these years, they've just given up on trying to change our minds.

I guess you could say we are stubborn. But we are also polite, and that makes a huge difference.

# Chapter 7

## Sharing the Road ...

## With Other Homeschoolers

It was so lovely to begin our life as homeschoolers. It almost felt as if we should be blasting some patriotic anthem from our Minivan speakers as we pulled out onto the road, exercising our rights as Americans to choose what education we thought was best for our family. We were joining a movement of like minded folks, and we were ready for the support and encouragement they would no doubt shower us with while we journeyed along the road with them.

Wait. Hold up. Hit the brakes. Swerve to the shoulder.

Support and encouragement? From fellow homeschoolers?

Unfortunately, *not always.*

In my homeschooling journey thus far, I've met people who are supportive and caring, encouraging and uplifting. They'll cheer you on, offer advice, and help you out. But every so often, I come across a homeschooling parent who seems bent on turning our differences as homeschoolers into World War Three.

And I don't get it.

Homeschoolers are a funny crew. We know that people homeschool for different reasons and in different ways. We say it all the time. But do we *really* get what that means?

It means the focus of every homeschool is different.

It means everyone's ideal homeschool life looks different.

It means we aren't carbon copies of each other, and the way and reason I homeschool has everything to do with me and nothing to do with you. So it means if I have decided to homeschool for religious reasons, I'm probably not going to be jealous of how free and relaxed my neighbor's homeschool is. If I'm homeschooling because of food allergies, I probably don't care how many field trips my cousins's homeschool goes on a week or what co-op my brother's kids go to. If the only reason I decided to homeschool is because of my husband's work schedule, it might not make a bit of difference to me that your kids are only doing real life math. If it works for you, that's great. Remember, your choice is perfect. But it has *nothing to do* with why I chose to homeschool. Your reasons might not even be on my radar.

Sometimes we get it so wrong. Comparing two homeschools (or two ways of homeschooling) to each other is not comparing apples to apples. It's more like trying to compare raspberries to dining room tables and celery to paint swatches. The two don't necessarily agree.

Do they have to?

We, as a group of homeschoolers, stepped away from the mainstream "normal" way of doing things for whatever reason. We believed our kids needed something different. We believed you can't lump every child together in a blob and try to educate them like carbon copies of each other, so we pulled out of the rat race and...

Well...

And...

We got over here to the homeschooling side of the fence and now spend our time arguing about...how all children should be unschooled? How if your kids use a desk you're basically copying school and have violated some unwritten homeschooling law? How one certain math curriculum is the only way children learn, and if you don't start with it, you'll just end up going back to it anyway?

Does anyone else see the blinding irony here?

If one-method-schooling is one of the biggest downfalls of public school, we shouldn't be so quick to turn homeschooling into the same exact thing with a different name.

## Labels are for soup cans

So often what this bickering boils down to is what kind of homeschooler you are, or what label you operate under.

Now on our Minivan of Awesome, we haven't slapped on any bumper stickers lately proclaiming what kind of homeschooler we are. In the beginning we did, but it never failed that a more enlightened and ultimately cooler Minivan would drive up and rip the bumper sticker off, claiming we were not doing the right things to proudly wear that bumper sticker.

It should have been a sign.

I don't pay a lot of attention to labels, for a few reasons. One, in my experience they don't help. Yes, labels can help us communicate something, but homeschooling labels are quite ambiguous. I heard a joke once that said if you ask 30 unschoolers what the definition of unschooling is, you'll get 45 answers. It is very hard to objectively define different methods of homeschooling and all the subsections underneath them.

I also don't give a lot of weight to labels because the longer I homeschool, the more the edges of those labels blur. The way we learn changes and morphs and goes back and moves forward. When you've been homeschooling long enough, you generally get comfortable in the Minivan you're driving and you know what works for your family and what will ensure a complete disaster. You seem to lose the need to define what kind of homeschooler you are.

But the most important reason I don't pay attention to labels anymore? My kids don't care one lick about them.

While I was preparing to speak at a conference one day, I asked my oldest, "Darling son, what kind of homeschoolers do you think we are?"

He looked at me like I had ten heads.

"What do you mean?" he asked.

"Well, you know. There are all sorts of different types of homeschoolers."

"There are?"

And as I went on to explain the differences between the labels, he stopped me and said something brilliant.

"We're not in public school. We learn at home. Isn't that what homeschooling is?"

For my kids, that's as far as it goes. They don't care (and yours probably don't either) what label we operate under or how well we fit some other homeschooler's definition of what that label is. If you ask my kids what an unschooler is or what Charlotte Mason education is or what a Waldorf-inspired homeschool is...they wouldn't be able to tell you. And they wouldn't care. Would yours? If not, then why do we spend nights awake trying to define what kind of homeschool we run?

You chose homeschooling for your kids and your family. Not the neighbor or the blogger you really admire or the librarian who homeschooled her kids twenty years ago. You do it for your family. So it shouldn't make a bit of difference what your neighbor, the blogger, or the librarian would classify you as.

If *we learn at home* works for my kids, it works for me, too.

## Compare, compete, and win

I remember back to very early in our journey when I visited a new homeschooling friend. Her daughters were older, and had displayed their cursive handwriting samples on the refrigerator. They were amazing! Fluid and fancy and gorgeous. I immediately thought of my own boys' handwriting which was nothing more than shaky printing at the time.

"Wow," I commented. "Looks like my boys really need to step it up in their handwriting."

She immediately giggled, shook her head and said, "Your boys are just barely learning to write. My girls are much older. Let it go!"

Handled perfectly. Not only did she not gloat about her children's amazing handwriting, she also cut me off from the comparing that (back then) I would have obsessed over for days.

What is it about our human nature that makes us want to compare and compete? And what is it about homeschooling that ramps up our comparative, competitive nature to dizzying heights?

I also remember, not long after that experience, my boys got penpals. I wanted so much for the boys to show what we'd been working on. Gosh, letter writing became stressful and I soon realized that them writing to their friends was not so much about them learning to write a letter as it was me wanting my kids to perform in an effort to prove I was teaching them something!

Naughty Mama! Since when did the Minivan become about me?

And then one day, the penpal sent a letter to my boys...and it was the best letter he'd ever sent. Why? He'd obviously sent it "just because" (the best reason to send a letter, right?) and probably without any help from his mom. Gone was the perfect spelling and the straight lines across the page he'd come to be known for. The grammar wasn't all that great...but you know what? My son understood it perfectly, enjoyed reading it, and sat down right there to return the letter.

I didn't worry about the spelling, letter spacing, or grammar so much after that. I realized writing a letter was a process, not a competition, and it wasn't necessary that I turned every single thing we encountered into a lesson.

I also realized that homeschooling is full of mindtraps, and the Compare and Compete trap will mess you up somethin' fierce. We feel the need to prove we're doing something, that homeschooling works, and that our kids will turn out ok. We want to show our mother-in-law we weren't nuts for choosing this life. We want to prove to ourselves that we can do this.

And while that in and of itself isn't necessarily terrible, sometimes it all comes out in nasty ways.

## People are watching...and they aren't all homeschoolers

Oh, the joys of social media. A place where people can hash out their disagreements and have everyone watch. What a voyeuristic society we are!

I am reminded of a social media conversation between two friends who homeschooled. They were on opposite ends of the homeschooling spectrum and generally couldn't talk about it without getting into some sort of argument. They spent a lot of time hashing out their differences (not very nicely, either) and I started to wonder if they kept each other on their friend lists just so they've have someone to bicker with.

One day, in the middle of a heated exchange about the merits of the opposite ways they homeschooled, a non-homeschooling friend interjected a comment:

"You know, it seems to me that the two of you spend more time arguing about homeschooling than actually doing it."

Ouch.

People are watching us. When we spend our time bickering about what lane of the Homeschooling Highway is better, people see that. What message are we sending to the world when they see so much bickering and arguing within a group that has separated in order to differently educate part of the future generation of Americans?

## We need your support

It's not our job to argue with each other about who is doing what right or wrong. Our job is to support each other in what we *are* doing, which is *homeschooling*.

If we don't stand up for each other, even if we homeschool differently, who will? Our sister who thinks we are nuts for choosing this lifestyle? The neighbor who asked if our kids needed a truancy officer? The PTA at the local public school?

I like to play Switzerland. I'm that mom who tries to get along  because I really believe in most cases, homeschooling parents just want to do what works best for their family and is best for their kids – even if that looks different than what is best for my family. But some people get so caught up in what works for them that they forget it won't work for everyone else.

That's not helping.

Arguing and bickering doesn't help. At all.

So many homeschoolers cite flexibility as a reason for homeschooling and yet forget that other people's family situations are not a cookie cutter version of their own home. Why are we telling people *I can't believe unschooling didn't work for you,* or *how could Charlotte Mason be boring for your kids* or *how can you possibly use desks like in a public school?* You *know* that doesn't sound supportive, right?

Something that often gets ignored by both sides is this simple point: the wrong way for your family *might actually work for someone else.* There is nothing more frustrating than to hop into the middle of a forum discussion where two people are throwing comments back and forth like "Without a schedule, he'll turn into a criminal" or "With a schedule, you're crushing his spirit!"

Come on, now. Can we stop swerving and trying to push each other off the road?

As a whole, homeschooling parents just want to do the best for the child and their education and that can present itself in many different forms. Some parents believe that unschooling (in its many, *many* different definitions) is the right choice for their family. If it works within their family and lifestyle, who is to say they are wrong? Other parents take a more structured approach because they believe it is the right choice for their family. If it works within their family and lifestyle, who is to tell them they wrong?

There will always be those people who want to debate everything. Maybe it pads their ego. Maybe it's a way for them to validate (to themselves or their watchful mother-in-law) the choice they made. And even though I find it hard to believe as a homeschooler, maybe they just have too much time on their hands!

Fellow drivers of Minivans of Awesome, let's remember we are lucky enough to have the "right" to step away from the public school system and have some freedom about how our children learn at home. Let's not waste our time setting up little camps of "my way is better". Homeschooling is about choice, and every homeschooler gets the freedom to make that choice.

I propose we all get new bumpers stickers that say "I support my fellow homeschooler." Agreed? Good.

Let's drive on!

# Chapter 8

## Riding Shotgun:

## How Homeschooling Affects Your Other Half

From the time my sons were quite little, I knew I wanted to homeschool. However, I wasn't the only adult in the Minivan of Awesome. I had some discussing and persuading to do of the man who would be sitting next to me for the duration of our trip.

My sweet husband must have thought I was nuts the first time I brought it up. Here was this crazed Jekyll and Hyde coming at him, half the time cooing, "Honey, I think we should homeschool!" and the other half flipping out at the kids (still in diapers at the time) for so much as *breathing* too loudly. I can't imagine *why* he didn't think me staying home with the kids forever and ever to be responsible for their education was anything less than the most stellar of ideas.

As you can see, I had a long way to go.

I'm glad he stuck with me to see it through.

This is the chapter that asks us to look in the mirror and be really honest about homeschooling and how it affects one particular Minivan relationship. This is about that person sharing the bench seat with you. The person who fiddles with the heater, changes the radio station, pumps your gas and helps keep you awake enough to drive when toothpicks won't help your eyelids.

Your spouse. In my case, and in the majority of homeschooling families, we're talking about hubby.

In writing this chapter, I spoke with several husbands of homeschooling moms. The names have been changed to protect them from their wives. (Kidding. Well...kind of.) I asked questions and I wasn't looking for canned, rehearsed, fluffy responses. I wanted honest answers. I wanted to know what they *really* thought about the trip in the Minivan of Awesome. What does homeschooling mean to them, as our partner in crime? Has homeschooling changed *us*? What kinds of things are going through their head? Let's be brave and get into what's really behind those eyes that sometimes glaze over when we're babbling about the difference between spelling curriculum A, B, and C.

## "I have to explain and defend everything you do."

We homeschoolers are so bold, right? We're tough as nails and we don't care what anyone thinks about our decision.

I have no doubt that when I announced I wanted to homeschool, people in my extended family didn't blink an eye. They asked questions and gave opinions, but homeschooling made sense coming from me. Homeschooling was different, and I'd always been the one who had to be different.

But my poor husband? Here I was dragging him through the muck of *your wife wants to do what* and *where in the world did she get that idea* and *you're not really going to let her do that, are you* and *why doesn't she just go out and get a real job?*

Here was this thing *I* wanted to do, and when people heard about it and started to ask questions, my husband had two options: Shake his head and walk away, or explain and defend his crazy wife.

Geez. And he could have married someone normal.

Here's the thing. When we mamas first decide we want to homeschool, we talk to people and research and read and talk to more people and find out everything we can about it. But if Dad isn't in on that research process, he probably doesn't know much about it at all. So he's got a ton of questions. He needs answers.

And he doesn't want his kids to be weird.

"Can I be honest?" Shawn, father of two boys, asked. "I just wanted to make sure my kids weren't going to be the weird ones getting pointed at and laughed at. No Dad wants that and I wanted to make sure we weren't choosing a lifestyle that was just going to make that more likely. Yeah, I feel stupid saying it now, because I know that's not how things really work. But that's what I was honestly thinking when my wife first brought the whole homeschooling thing up. And I'd be willing to bet that's what lots of other dads worry about, too."

Yes, I know it's almost like going backwards in this book. We've already hashed out what other people think of us. But in the beginning when Dad doesn't know or understand homeschooling, his questions or opinions might not be all that different from what all those other people think. And Dad is much closer to the situation at hand.

So we need to convince him his kids aren't going to be weird.

Or at least any weirder than they already are.

We need to show Dad that other people are homeschooling, not just (insert stereotypical thing he's heard about people who homeschool that you obviously aren't). I had the perfect opportunity to do this at a local "Information Station" put on by the Minnesota Homeschoolers' Alliance. It was a gathering led by veteran homeschoolers who simply explained to newcomers how to enter the big scary world of homeschooling, and then answered their many questions.

My husband and I called it date night, and went to this gathering. There were gobs of people. All of them looking quite normal. Just...normal. And they all asked normal questions.

Normal. Just what my husband needed to be convinced of.

Now, I don't know if he realizes it, but his entire demeanor towards homeschooling changed immediately after that meeting. You could see it in his posture. You could hear it in how he suddenly talked about all our future plans. It was no longer a question of *will people think we are weird*. The question now was *when can we start?*

### "You and the kids are like a secret society."

The togetherness of homeschooling is fabulous...but not if you're on the outside looking in. Shawn says he often feels isolated from his family.

"It's the weirdest thing," he admitted. "Because I thought homeschooling would bring us closer together as a family. But what I ended up actually feeling was that my wife and boys had a little secret society full of things I didn't get. Inside jokes, references to things they'd done without me...they have a "thing", and I'm not a part of it. I kind of feel like I am always a couple steps behind."

Has your family unknowingly created a little subculture that Dad doesn't understand or can't get into? We have to make sure we aren't isolating Dad. When my boys were much younger and my husband's work schedule was really crazy, the boys and I would make sure we wrote down a list of what we'd done that day so he knew how we'd spent our time. Then when my husband would get home, they'd hand him this very special piece of paper, they'd read it together and then talk about it. It worked well, because in the craziness of our day, by the time Dad got home, we'd forget to fill him in on school. And if Dad didn't hear about that part of our day, for many days in a row, there was a whole bunch he suddenly didn't know about how his family was living their life.

Yes, togetherness is great and it's good to know what's going on. But having said that, I also think it is really important that your spouse has a "thing" with your kids that you aren't a part of...especially as your kids get older. I'm a backwoods Minnesota girl. I like to hunt, fish, and build things. You would think those are perfect skills to have as the mom of boys. And they are. But I also know it's important my boys have *their time* and *their thing* with Dad that has *nothing* to do with me. Even though I enjoy hunting, fishing, and building things, there are times I back out because the boys sometimes need me *not* to be there. And so does my husband.

Kids are different when spending time with just mom or just dad, and that's ok. In a homeschool setting, it's really important that the kids get that time with the *other* parent. Not to give you a break, necessarily, but so the kids don't experience the majority of their life with only one half of the whole.

Homeschooling is the epitome of togetherness, but if played incorrectly, the balance can get totally messed up.

Jim, another homeschooling dad of all boys said, "You never realize how close Mom and the boys will get, and how much you *won't be there for* during the day. If my wife was working and the boys were in public school, we'd all sit around the dinner table at night and talk about our days and it would be fine. But when most the people around the table have already been together all day, it's not the same kind of conversation."

Jim went on to explain he felt that *his* life, homeschooling or not, wasn't any different. He was still working a 9-5 job away from home either way. What he did feel different about with homeschooling, however, was the atmosphere inside their home.

"It's calmer, I think," he said. "And the kids aren't as withdrawn from each other or the family as my co-workers complain about with their kids. But then it's ironic how because of their togetherness, I feel less a part of them and what they have. Maybe it's jealousy?"

Jealousy. Hear that? And we spend our time complaining that the kids are loud and messy?

**"You're teaching the kids in a way I don't agree with."**

Sometimes the issue is not so much that life is grand and Dad is jealous he can't be there to see it. Instead, sometimes the issue is that Dad doesn't agree with what is going on or how it's all happening.

"Yes, I agreed to this homeschooling business," said Joshua, father of three. "(My wife) kind of sold it to me as this packaged-up thing of great academics and responsibility. But once she got into it...I kid you not...my three were running around crazy all the time. My seven year old couldn't write her name. My ten year old asked me if the money she'd saved from her birthday (twenty dollars) was enough to buy the $13.95 game she had picked out at the store. *How* can you tell me homeschooling is a productive choice for us?"

It's quite possible for mom and dad to agree on the concept of homeschooling, but not the method. Elijah, father of one whose wife had just started homeschooling, said, "My wife really wanted to run things more relaxed. Unschooling, I guess you call it. I told her I thought the concept was great, but that I also didn't see anything wrong with our daughter sitting down and learning to write a letter. Or add money. My wife thinks our daughter should learn that when she wants to. I told my wife that standing in line at the grocery store with ten people behind you is not the place to finally teach our daughter how many quarters will buy her a candy bar."

"I'm just afraid my kids are going to be totally disillusioned with life," Joshua continued. "There are some things in life you just have to do. That's real life. My wife is determined to cocoon our kids into thinking the world is their playground. When they are little...ok, I get that. But my thirteen year old wants to go to college for video game design. Tell me...when his professor asks him to write a paper or do a test...what is my son going to do? He's never had to do anything like that yet. Will he just...all of a sudden know how to do it?"

Sometimes Dad isn't so concerned about the lack of structure as they are the lack of freedom.

"I'm tired of my wife running our house like a brick and mortar," William, father of five, complained. "We are homeschooling. If I wanted to see a daily schedule on the wall, complete with a timer as a school bell, I would have trudged the kids down the street to the local elementary. I just wish she'd lighten up."

"She's always in teacher mode," agreed Shawn. "It's bad enough to feel isolated from the family, but then I feel like I crawl into bed with Teacher, not Wife."

Now, the point is not who you agree with here, or if you agree with any of them. The point is that the gentlemen and ladies did not agree on the methods for teaching. And regardless of where you hang out in the homeschooling spectrum, disagreements in the front seat of the Minivan can make the ride a whole lot more stressful.

Oh. And speaking of stressful...

**"You're always around the kids...so you're always stressed out."**

Well, all righty then.

Believe it or not, some form of "she's crabby" is what I hear the most when I really get husbands talking about their homeschooling wives.

*Pshaw*, you're thinking. *Whatever. I'm sweet as honey after trying to explain the scientific method to an eleven year old who would rather be playing Zelda.*

I'm sure you are. I mean, I know *I am*, so I'm sure *you are*.

Ahem.

Among the husbands I've talked with over the past couple years, some were concerned about the stress level homeschooling moms were experiencing, while others were flat out tired of being the target of mom's constant frustration. Dan, father of four, said, "I never doubted that homeschooling was academically the best choice for our family. But relationship wise? Stress wise? My wife turned into a complete raging nutcase."

I'm sure we have *no* idea what he's talking about.

Ok. In all seriousness, we know that we can get crabby. Stressed out. Even raging nutcase-like. Because in all honesty, trying to teach a lot of things to our kids could put us in a straight jacket. But to consistently freak out at our husband because we're stressed out? Probably not the best way to handle it. He's on our team, remember? Why are we taking everything out on him? Especially when the choice to bring the family into this lifestyle was (drumroll...) nine times out of ten *our* choice?

**"You got what you wanted, but all you do is complain about it."**

I've known homeschooling moms who spend their time absolutely livid at their husbands because "they aren't helping with the homeschooling". One dad responded with,

"I fund, you teach." Another blunt dad said "If you don't like the arrangement, send the kids to public school."

And you wonder why I changed their names.

But I get it. The problem is we are teaching *our kids*. These aren't some random hoodlums off the street. These kids belong to Dad, too, and we want him to be involved.

Here's the thing, though. Yes, homeschooling moms work hard and I would be the last person to discredit that. I know what it's like to want to pull your hair out over math, science, and spelling. But I also know what it's like to work in construction, siding houses and putting on roofs. If I still worked a day like that, dragged my butt home, and then got yelled at for not being there to teach math, I'd probably tell my spouse to put the kids on the big yellow bus the next day.

Seriously.

Sometimes we forget that we asked and prayed and hoped for the opportunity and set-up that would make homeschooling possible for our family.

Amazingly enough, we got it.

We got it, and then...that's right...we *complained* about it.

*Hey, wait!* you're saying. *Weren't you the one that said we shouldn't be afraid to talk about the hard parts?*

Yes. About that.

It's one thing to blow off a little steam. I am not from the school of Put Up and Shut Up, so I've been known to toss out a few grunts and groans when the Minivan gets stuffy and hard to steer. Occasional grunts and groans are normal, not to mention healthy! We all have things that bug us about the dailyness and hard work of homeschooling, and we should be able to talk about those. I don't think our spouse, friends, or fellow homeschoolers have any problems listening to our occasional gripes.

But that's not what I'm referring to. There is a line between getting something off your chest and lamenting the hardships of your choice on a daily...or hourly...or by-the-minute basis. I'm talking about the people who incessantly complain and point out the negatives in every possible homeschooling situation. The people who choose to homeschool and then dedicate all their time to talking about how horribly terrible it is.

You *know* the people I'm talking about.

If your sister calls to tell you about the great new job she's taken (the one she's always wanted), but fills the first ten minutes of conversation with only negative comments about it, wouldn't you wonder *why* she'd chosen to take that job?

I sure would. And it's the same thing with homeschooling. When your spouse agrees to That Homeschooling Thing after a year of hint dropping and eye batting, but then spends the next year listening to you complain about how hard it is, how you never get any time away from your kids, and how you've lost yourself...don't you think he might be wondering why on earth you chose to take this job? And, if it's so terrible, why you don't choose something else?

Homeschooling is a choice. I've said it many times in this book, and I'll keep saying it until people really understand what it means. Homeschooling is a choice.

Which brings us to our next issue.

### "I wasn't the one who chose to do this."

There is a difference between two people making a choice together, and one person *supporting* another person's choice. Ever heard the Minivan of Awesome cough and sputter? It might be because one person thought the trip was a team decision, and the other thought they were simply supporting the other party's wishes to take it.

Big difference.

Brian, father of three, shared the story of his wife deciding to take on a part time job. What he didn't realize, however, was that she suddenly thought he was going to take on half of the homeschooling responsibility because she was now bringing in an income.

"We had a huge fight about it," he said. "She assumed that our individual teaching responsibilities were directly related to how much money we were bringing into the house. As if the reason she had been doing all the teaching was because she wasn't working outside the home. I reminded her that the reason she was doing all the teaching was because *she was the one who chose to homeschool*."

Jon, another father of three, found himself in a similar situation. He said, "I told my wife I didn't mind helping the kids with stuff, because if they were in public school I'd already be helping them with homework. But to assume that since she was now pulling an income that I'd suddenly come home from work and do enormous science experiments or some giant music curriculum every night? No. Homeschooling was her choice, not mine. I supported her, but it wasn't my choice to *do it*."

When my husband and I had our final discussion about whether or not homeschooling was right for our family, he was very excited and supportive. But let's be honest: he ended the conversation with "If you think you can handle it, I think it's worth a try."

If **you** think **you** can handle it...

The man I married is a wonderful father and a supportive husband. He's more than happy to offer suggestions when I'm struggling with how to teach something. He's sat with the kids and explained things to them in ways I can't. He's my go-to-guy when I can't figure out how to put an experiment together.

But he's not the teacher. He didn't sign up for homeschooling. He simply supported me in *my* desire to do it.

Sometimes Dad's involvement is the funding. And sometimes our involvement is the teaching. He's focusing on the funding so we can focus on the teaching. At the end of the day they are equally as important. Homeschooling can't happen without both of them in place.

*But hey,* you're saying. *I'm not a one income household! I work, too!* Or *I'm a one income household because I'm a single parent!*

True, not everyone has a "traditional" home set up. Statistics show it's common among homeschoolers, but not a hard and fast rule. In the end, however, the decision to take a ride in the Minivan of Awesome is all about choice, regardless of where your income comes from. Every homeschool has its own set up, path, and struggles. But at the end of the day, whether you're rolling in the dough or pinching pennies, it's still a choice to be there.

Homeschooling is family affair and we need to make sure all riders in the Minivan are happily boppin' along with the bumps. Our biggest supporter and the one who will cheer for us loudest needs to be treated as the person sitting beside us, not someone sitting on the shoulder watching the Minivan go by. He's contributing to the Homeschool Thing in ways we aren't...and they are just as important. We need to remember, when it is all said and done, homeschooling is a choice. It's *always* a choice. And if at some point it isn't working anymore...perhaps it's time to make a different one.

# Chapter 9

## Take The Next Exit:

## Sometimes Homeschooling Doesn't Work Out

If homeschooling is a choice, and the choice isn't working, it's time to choose something else.

For all the millions of advantages of homeschooling, for all the wonderful things homeschooling does, there's one thing you can't ignore.

Sometimes, it just doesn't work out.

And that's ok.

And yes, I *did* just say that.

Life in the Minivan of Awesome is more than just choosing a curriculum or classifying yourself as an unschooler. It has a lot to do with home environment, schedules, personalities...and a great many things that are completely out of your control. Homeschooling invades a lot of places in your headspace that you aren't aware of until you're already buckled in for the ride. Homeschooling can do a lot, but it can also *be* too much.

"We homeschooled for seven years," Jenna, homeschooling mom of four, told me. "Things were fine in the beginning. We were really enjoying it. But in year six, something changed. I don't know if we've ever figured out what it was, but homeschooling just became this daily struggle of personalities and relationships and wants and needs and I couldn't do it anymore."

Erin, homeschooling mom of one, taught her daughter for one year. "I'm pretty sure I struggled with my daughter every last one of those days. It was constant personality clashes. I'm serious, *every* day. I don't think I was ever cut out to homeschool. And I'm ok with that."

"I just didn't feel like I had anything left to give my kids," said Amanda, mom of three. "And that's when I knew it was time for us to be done homeschooling. We were always crabby at each other. I wasn't willing to sacrifice our home life in order to say I was homeschooling."

I've met several families in my time on the Homeschooling Highway. Some finish out the road, some take an exit, some return, and some don't. There's always a reason for if they go or if they stay.

"Financially, we were in trouble," another mom said. "My husband lost his job and was unemployed for months. I was offered a job that would help us keep afloat. But I didn't feel I could have that particular job and do the homeschooling, too. So my husband took over the homeschooling. But three months later, he was offered an opportunity to go back to school to finish up his degree and find better work. Just like that, our entire household setup had changed. Our kids all went back to public school. And you know what? We survived."

Everyone who has tried their time on the Homeschooling Highway and ultimately taken an exit off has their own story about why it didn't work for them. And I'm always interested in hearing people's stories. But what's most interesting to me about those stories is when those who have exited the Highway talk about how their exit was received by those who were still on it.

### Shunned...by a homeschooler?

"When we put our kids back in school, there were a few of my friends who didn't care," said Amanda. "I still talk to some of them. But for the most part I really felt it was inferred that I'd failed at homeschooling and I was totally screwing my kids up by sending them back into the public school system."

Well, now. That's pleasant, isn't it?

"It was ridiculous," agreed Erin. "I mean, I get that if we aren't homeschooling, there's a part of our life that we don't have in common anymore. But really? I felt like when I put my daughter in school, it was like I was being shunned. Like people didn't know what to talk to me about anymore. You know, because there was this whole school thing in the way."

I'm stumped with this one. Fellow drivers of Awesome Minivans, why are we looking down at people who decide homeschooling isn't their thing? If homeschooling is all about choice, why do we put our noses up when someone *chooses not* to homeschool? I've always admired parents who are strong enough to take an honest look at their family, realize something isn't working, and opt for something else. If it's ok for Awesome Minivans to do it to the public school, why is it so hard to accept when someone does it to homeschooling?

The most ironic display of homeschool shunning I've heard of, however, was Beth, a self-proclaimed radical unschooler who had two of five children announce they wanted to try public school.

"I'm still an unschooler," Beth said, proudly. "Unschooling is about following your children's desires. Letting them be in charge of where they want to go. If they want to try a year of public school, why should I tell them no?"

She believed she was doing something awesome for her kids. But the backlash? The emails? The comments?

"Other homeschoolers were furious that I would do that. They were appalled that I'd even consider letting my kids try public school. I asked all those people what they were afraid of. That one or all of my kids would actually like public school? And...so what if they did?"

### Public school: press like?

Many of the people I run into who don't homeschool seem to think all homeschoolers are anti-public school.

That's simply not true.

The problem is there are also many people who homeschool who believe that all homeschoolers *should be* anti-public school. You know, because public school is evil. The work of Satan. The downfall of American society.

You get the idea.

I suppose if you believe homeschooling is The Way and The Choice (instead of A Way and A Choice), you're going to frown upon anyone leaving the fold. But for those of us (author included) whose choice to homeschool had nothing to do with a belief about the very core of the public school system being putrid and worthless, there isn't the same aversion to students "going back".

I believe, as many homeschoolers I've met, that there *are* good teachers to be found in the public school system. There *are* schools that are trying. There *are* people who are working for the kids. I think when we throw the baby out with the public school bathwater, we're doing a real disservice to both the public school and homeschoolers.

Not to mention our kids.

I know that most of us start off homeschooling with wonderful intentions, planning a homeschool grad party that will be oh-so-cool at the end of the road. But not all of us get there, for as many reasons as there are people, and our kids might end up at (gasp!) the public school.

Here is something to ponder: if we spend all our time badmouthing the public school, how in the world can we expect our kids to cheerfully *attend* the public school if need be?

We don't know where life is going to take us. We don't know where our individual highways lead to. Dealing with life requires choices, and choices require options. We need to make sure we keep all our options open.

Badmouthing public school in ginormous sweeping statements also makes relationships hard for your kids. When all your kids ever hear about is how public school is terrible (doesn't work, turns out bad kids, is full of teachers who don't care, etc.), how do you expect them to react to their friends/cousins/scoutmates/park buddies who aren't homeschooled?

Let's be realistic, shall we? The world of education is big enough for all of us, and I guarantee you we all have much better things to do than fight. Public school isn't any closer to *evil* than homeschooling is to *perfect*.

### "You have to be educated somewhere, but…"

"I remember being so tired of her attitude," said Erin. "She walked around like the world belonged to her, and like I *had* to homeschool her. Like I *had* to put up with her attitude."

One of the questions often asked of homeschooling parents is *how long do you plan to homeschool your kids*? And while some people have an actual timeline in place, our answer is always *we will homeschool as long as it works for our family*.

I don't see anything wrong with laying out the facts for your kids. There have been several conversations in our house when things have gotten particularly sticky, about what the phrase *works for our family* means. My children, because of those conversations, are now well versed in the fact they a) are legally required to be educated in some manner, but b) we are not legally required to have that education take place at home. Everyone's assistance and cooperation is required to keep the education happening at our lil' five acre farm and not at the brick building in town.

My oldest was seven years old the first time we had this conversation. Many people thought it was far too adult of a conversation to have with him. I disagreed. I wanted my kids to know there were reasons we had chosen homeschooling for our family, but that there were no absolutes. If at any time it seemed to be not working for someone in the family, it meant it wasn't working for the family as a whole. We are in the Minivan of Awesome *together,* and *together* dictates the decisions we make. The option is always there to re-evaluate, and if need be, choose something else.

Homeschooling is a process. Homeschooling is a journey. It is not always the final answer. (And if it isn't for your family, it doesn't mean you've failed!) Homeschooling gives the opportunity to figure out the way to learn and move towards what is right for that child and that family. Homeschooling is sometimes your Forever, and sometimes it is only your Right Now. Your ride in the Minivan of

Awesome, no matter how long or short, is worth the time you spent. Whatever your choice is, my friend, you've done well.

# Conclusion:

## Still Driving

So here I am. Still tooling down the Homeschooling Highway. After the last nine chapters of road bumps and car sickness...what sane person would choose to continue the journey?

Wait. Don't answer that...

We need to be aware that the Homeschooling Highway has sharp edges and pokey points and that we are never (ever!) guaranteed a nicely cushioned window seat.

But we *are* guaranteed a ride.

When you choose to buckle up for a drive on the Homeschooling Highway, you might be committing to insanity and all sorts of ridiculousness, but you're also signing up for togetherness and freedom and a flexibility in your life that's hard to find anywhere else.

In the last nine chapters, I've talked about the tough parts of homeschooling. I've plowed you through the potholes along the road. I think we are *all* farther ahead when we know what we might be in for than if we blindly put the Minivan in gear and hope we don't crash and burn.

We need to be prepared. We need to know what could be around the corner or up over the hill so we aren't blindsided by the roadblocks and detours that weren't on the map.

You've probably read it somewhere in this book already, but homeschooling is a choice. And every single day I'm reminded somehow of why we made the choice we did. I'm encouraged...and then I know why I'm still hanging out on the Homeschooling Highway. I'm supported...and remember why I'm still grinding through the gears in the Minivan of Awesome.

I hope this book has been an encouragement to you. I hope nine chapters of someone's reality in one corner of the homeschooling world has given you the confidence and support you need to look at your own journey in a very real way.

You're steering your own Minivan.

You're on your own path.

Make it work for you!

This is truly an awesome trip. It's an unforgettable experience to be on the road of homeschooling...even if we have to deal with road hogs, potholes, and occasional carsickness.

Enjoy the ride, fellow drivers.

*Enjoy the ride.*

## About The Author

Amy Dingmann lives on a multigenerational farm in Minnesota with her husband, two children, and her parents. She enjoys writing in the hayloft after a crazy day of homeschooling. Amy Dingmann has written for several magazines, both online and print. She also speaks to parenting and homeschooling groups. You can find her itty bitty piece of the online writing world at the following places:

*The Hmmmschooling Mom*

www.thehmmmschoolingmom.blogspot.com

*A Farmish Kind of Life*

www.farmfoodmama.blogspot.com

*Her author website*

www.amydingmann.com

Look for Amy's humorous fiction work to be released early 2013 (as Shay Ray Stevens).